100 UPLIFTING STORIES FOR SENIORS

Funny and True Easy to Read Short Stories to Stimulate the Mind

Charlie Miller

ISBN: 978-1-64845-093-8

CONTENTS

INTRODUCTION

Listen up: Have you heard a funny, inspiring, or upbeat story recently? If not, here they are: 100 uplifting stories, especially for the elderly and you. The basic aim of these stories is to make elderly people (and their dear families and caretakers) happier - while they deal with the many challenges of being seniors.

Some of the stories herein may even result in people laughing out loud. That's the point - because when you laugh, you and those around you feel better. Research has shown that reminiscing and good storytelling have many positive effects on seniors, in particular elevating their moods and sense of well-being, while also reducing agitation.

What's more: the heartwarming stories here are all true. They're written up to give you a boost. Enjoy and share them - and keep your spirits high.

CHAPTER 1:

ONE MAN, CONVICTED WRONGLY, FREES ANOTHER

Did you ever dream of becoming a lawyer? Remember all those great TV programs and movies about keeping law and order? They make the job seem really exciting. But to be a lawyer, you need to study a whole lot, and it costs a bunch of money to go to law school.

However, what if you were in prison, and you had A LOT of time on your hands? Like 28 years, to be more specific. Maybe then you could finally realize your dream of studying day and night to be a lawyer. That's exactly what happened to a man named Jarrett Adams, sentenced to almost three decades in the slammer for a crime he didn't actually commit.

Without going into too much detail about the actual crime, let's just say that Adams, from Chicago's South Side, went to a party in another state, Wisconsin, just before he was heading off to Junior College in 1998. He was a babe in the woods, so to speak, at age 17.

Suddenly he was arrested after an incident at the party and whisked back to Wisconsin where he couldn't afford legal support. A court-appointed lawyer advised him not to put up a defense - even though there was a witness who could've helped him off the hook.

Lucky for Adams, he met a cellmate who worked in the prison library who said, "Listen, I go over hundreds of inmate cases, and all of them say the same thing: 'I'm innocent.' But I've never seen a case like yours before."

You know very well that persistence is a virtue, so Adams never stopped studying and fighting for justice. The cellmate advised him not to surrender: "It's only going to take a second before you have tattoos on your face, and have given up completely, and don't care at all. You need to go down swinging," he said.

Cut to the present: we find Jarrett Adams as an attorney who recently helped overturn another innocent man's conviction - in the same state that sentenced him to prison for a crime he didn't commit many moons ago.

"This is a storybook," Adams exclaimed, "it's a storybook tale that you wouldn't believe until you saw it, to have a conviction overturned, and in a court, in a state, that I was wrongfully convicted." The case was Adams's first professional win and an extremely personal one for the 36-year-old. He spent almost a decade behind bars himself after a wrongful conviction.

"Successful men and women keep moving. They make mistakes, but they don't quit," Conrad Hilton once claimed.

CHAPTER 2:

PARALYZED VICTIM REGAINS UPPER BODY MOVEMENT AFTER STEM CELL TREATMENT

This book is full of uplifting stories, so perhaps you're surprised to hear that this second one is about a car crash in March 2016 that left a young man named Kristopher (Kris) Boesen unable to move from the neck down.

Following the accident, Kris even had a hard time breathing on his own - something that many of us take for granted. Due to the extent of his injuries, the victim was informed that he might never be able to control his arms and legs again.

The options that lay in front of Kris: try the typical surgery that most patients who suffer a severe spinal cord injury undergo (which would make his spine more stable but would probably do nothing to restore his motor functions and senses).

Or Kris could enroll with other patients like him in a study where stem cell injections were used to shrink the size of the injury cavity, boost nerve cell growth, and create blood vessels that deliver oxygen and healing in general to the injury.

Kris chose the second option, but then he had to show he was able to breathe on his own to take part in the trial. So, with the assistance and care of his hard-working respiratory team helped him breathe without a ventilator, and he was ultimately approved to participate.

Every year, there are about 17,000 cases of recent spinal cord injury in the USA, says the National Spinal Cord Injury Statistical Center. The stem cell treatment then appears to bring new hope to sufferers of such trauma. To those who believed they would never feel the pleasure of moving their limbs freely again, this study is but one instance that shows how regenerative medicine can deliver them from despair.

After only three weeks of therapy, Kris began to demonstrate clear signs of improvement. After two months, it appeared as if a miracle had happened. He was able to answer the phone, write his name, and get around a bit by himself in a wheelchair.

In addition, Kris's motor functions (controlled by messages sent from the brain to the various muscle groups) had also begun to function better. Your motor functions are what allow you to move, walk and swim, shake hands with your friends, and hug your family, so this made a huge difference.

CHAPTER 3:

HOLLYWOOD STAR SECRETLY FINANCES KIDS' HOSPITALS

If you happened to see the movie, *The Matrix*, you may remember a cool-looking guy with sunglasses who was able to bend backwards and sideways to avoid speeding bullets that somehow miraculously missed him, all in slow motion.

If you thought that was cool, wait until you hear what Hollywood superstar Keanu Reeves is doing now: He´s financing kids' hospitals. But not too many people know about it because Keanu is a relatively quiet guy (depending on which movie you saw). He normally lets his actions do the talking.

If you want to know more about Reeves, let's start with the fact that his dad has Chinese-Hawaiian, English, Irish, and Portuguese ancestors (we can only wonder what kind of food he likes best). Keanu decided on his first large donation to charity when his younger sister Kim was found to have leukemia in the 90s. Reeves became his sister's primary caretaker.

On top of his several donations to cancer charities, the *Matrix* main man started a foundation in his sister Kim´s honor, without putting his name on it. The organization helps pay for cancer research as well as supporting children´s wards.

"I have a private foundation that's been running for five or six years, and it helps aid a couple of children's hospitals and cancer research," Reeves told the media in 2009. "I don't like to attach my name to it. I just let the foundation do what it does."

When you're making millions as a movie star, it might seem easy, but Reeves also served as a volunteer on the Stand Up to Cancer telethon back in 2008. He also volunteered to go in goal during a charity ice hockey game called SCORE (Spinal Cord Opportunities for Rehabilitation Endowment).

What about on set - is Reeves a notoriously difficult actor to work with? According to sources, Keanu is as generous and kind on set as he is off.

"Every day for the last few weeks of filming, Keanu treated the stagehands and grunt workers (including myself) by taking us out for free breakfast and lunch," a Reddit user who worked on *Chain Reaction* with Reeves gushed. "He was genuinely a very nice guy to work with. Since then, I've worked on about 30 different sets, and have never met an actor who is as generous and friendly as him."

CHAPTER 4:

BELGIUM SAYS 'YES' TO A FOUR-DAY WEEK, AND EMPLOYEES CAN IGNORE BOSSES

Maybe you're already retired, and possibly you don't live in Belgium either. But we can guarantee that during your working life, you definitely dreamed about enjoying a four-day week. And we're willing to bet the ranch on the fact that, a few times at least, you most certainly wanted to totally ignore your boss.

Now, in Belgium, workers are allowed to do those two things. The country´s always been known for its great beer, but early in 2022, the multi-party coalition government there announced a package of reforms. It included the right of employees to turn off devices, and not pay any attention to messages related to their jobs after hours - and most importantly, without fear of punishment.

"We have experienced two difficult years. With this agreement, we set a beacon for an economy that is more innovative, sustainable, and digital. The aim is to be able to make people and businesses stronger," Alexander de Croo, Belgium´s prime minister, announced at a press conference about the reforms.

Nowadays, we have something called the 'gig economy' where certain workers do specific jobs for shorter periods. They'll also have stronger legal protections under Belgium's new rules, and full-time workers will enjoy the opportunity to work flexible schedules on demand.

It´s all about work-life balance now. Gone are the days of working your fingers to the bone, with Belgium and its positive reforms leading the way, and other countries soon to follow. You won´t be able to exactly tell your boss "take this job and shove it." But at the same time, the head honcho needs to leave you alone after hours too.

CHAPTER 5:

BILLIONAIRE GIVES AWAY COMPANY

If you're a billionaire, it's pretty easy to give away just about whatever you want (and then get a bigger and better one tomorrow). But in this particular case, Yvon Chouinard, the founder of the outdoor apparel brand Patagonia (worth billions), said he's giving away his company to a trust that will use its ample profits to fight the climate crisis.

Instead of selling the company, or taking it public, Chouinard (who became famous for steep climbs in Yosemite National Park and has a net worth of a cool $1.2 billion), has decided to transfer his family's control of the company to a trust along with a non-profit organization.

The climate crisis isn't too much fun, with temperatures rising, making us all a bit hot under the collar, and more extreme storms battering the places we know and love. "Each year, the money we make after reinvesting in the business will be distributed as a dividend to help fight the crisis," the Patagonia boss detailed in an open letter on the company website in September 2022.

"Instead of extracting value from nature, and transforming it into wealth for investors, we'll use the wealth Patagonia creates to protect the source of all wealth," Yvon explained. In addition, according to those in the know at the *New York Times*, the structure of the Patagonia founder's action made it clear that he and his family would enjoy no financial benefits. Indeed, the Chouinards would face a hefty tax bill from this donation.

That's a bit different from a lot of rich fat cats who contribute to causes specifically to avoid paying taxes.

Thanks a lot, Yvon.

CHAPTER 6:

NEWARK POLICE FIRE NO SHOTS IN 2020

You've got to admit that being a police officer is not easy, especially in a roughneck place like Newark, New Jersey. Then you´d be hard-pressed to believe that during the entire year of 2020, the police force in Newark didn't fire a single shot - and their guns were working just fine.

That's because of a new de-escalation program designed to fight crime - not exactly with flowers - but with fewer or no bullets. Believe it or not, this exemplary behavior by the Newark crime fighters happened in one of the most trying years on record. Public Safety Director Anthony Ambrose claimed that 2020 was the toughest year in his 34-year career in law enforcement.

All told, six of the 1,100 Newark officers lost their lives to Covid-19 during the period, while dozens more got sick after being exposed on the job. The force faced major obstacles during the summer's anti-police brutality protests as well, related to the tension surrounding George Floyd´s untimely death.

But through it all, Ambrose remarked that not a single officer in the city discharged his or her weapon while on duty in 2020. "It was the unknown. It was the unknown that you didn't know with this disease that you were coming here every day, and these police officers and firefighters going out there, and we didn't know," says Ambrose.

Like many public servants around the world, for Newark police, 2020 was a year of Covid fears, high hurdles, and losses. "We lost six police officers, and going to six funerals, it all wears on you," Ambrose recalls.

It´s never been easy in Newark, but in 2020, the officers there wore it well.

CHAPTER 7:

PORTUGAL DECLARES BOSSES CAN'T TEXT YOU AFTER WORK

You've already heard about Belgium in this book. But now, if you're just settling down to a delectable codfish meal, and maybe even tasting some delicious local wine with your dish somewhere on the coast of Portugal, your boss can't bug you with text messages anymore. Sorry, Mr. Head Honcho, you're just going to have to take a backseat to our proper nutrition.

Remote workers in Portugal should see a better work-life balance under the new labor laws approved recently by that country's parliament. The new rules approved are a clear response to the explosion of home or remote working resulting from the Covid-19 pandemic, the country's ruling Socialist Party said.

According to the new rules, employers might face penalties for contacting workers outside office hours. Out of curiosity: we´re very anxious to know if the penalties could include bosses delivering a slab of Portugal´s world-famous codfish to affected workers!

Companies will also have to help pay for expenses directly related to remote working - higher electricity and internet bills come immediately to mind (but you´ll still need to pay for your own water use). Just to let you know: the amendments to Portugal's labor laws do have certain limits. They will not apply to companies with fewer than 10 workers.

The new rules also provide some positive news for parents of young kids. They now have the right to work from home without the need to arrange it beforehand with their employers - at least up until their youngster turns eight years old.

Finally, there are actions designed to tackle loneliness also included in the remote working rules. Companies are expected to set up face-to-face meetings every two months at least.

Just in case you´re really missing your boss´s jokes, and advice on areas in which you can improve, in person, you´ll still get an earful every odd month in Portugal.

CHAPTER 8:

NO KIDS KILLED IN NORWAY TRAFFIC ACCIDENTS IN 2019

What on earth are they doing right in Oslo, Norway, so that no kids at all were killed in traffic accidents there during the whole year of 2019? In fact, only one person of any age died on that fair city´s roads during the year in question (at the same time, 126 perished on the highways and byways of London - though to be fair, the latter city is considerably bigger). Population – Oslo 2022 – 1,071,000 and population London 2022 – 9,541,000.

Even so, the UK is considered one of the safest countries in the European Union for traffic accidents, with fewer than 30 fatalities per million inhabitants. And can you guess the two European countries considered the most dangerous in terms of traffic deaths? If you guessed Bulgaria and Romania, you´re right on target.

Norway has been focused on a plan called Vision Zero since 2002. Two key factors for the country´s outstanding safety record are reduced speeds on the Nordic country´s roads, and cars that have as many safety features as you and I can ever imagine.

The Oslo city administration established limits in driving zones, particular in the city center, and went about establishing plenty of seamless cycling lanes to incentivize citizens to get around on two wheels instead of four. (We can only imagine that folks get around there on skis in winter when bike riding gets more challenging, due to the abundant snow and ice.)

Vision Zero is a scheme adopted by other EU member states as well, including the United Kingdom. Back to our friends in London, Mayor Sadiq Khan says he plans to make 80% of all trips in the capital car-free by 2041. This is an ambitious part of the city´s transport tactics, all in line with such a vision of zero deaths, along with lots of happy parents and pedestrians.

CHAPTER 9:

CHECK YOUR OLD SHIRT, AND WIN THE LOTTERY

How many times have you heard the old saying, "You can't win the lottery if you don't buy a ticket!" Probably a few hundred times, at the very least. But now, there's a new saying going around: "If you want to win the lottery, and retire on the beach, you need to first buy a ticket, and then, make sure to check the pocket of your old shirt."

That was the magic formula for Jimmie Smith who happened to find an old ticket worth a few bucks ($24 million to be precise) in the pocket of his shirt "just in the nick of time" back in 2017.

Most folks have a place where mail and a few pieces of scrap paper perhaps pile up. For 68-year-old Jimmie Smith, it turned out to be an old shirt dangling in his closet. Somehow stuffed in its pocket was a nice stash of unconfirmed lottery tickets.

"I always told myself, 'I'll check them when I have the time,'" admitted the New Jersey resident. We're sure glad he did because if he'd waited two days more, he'd have missed out on a grand total of $24.1 million.

A full year before, Smith splurged on a ticket to the New York Lotto. Just in case you're tempted to try the same numbers, Jimmie's clinching combo for May 25, 2016, game was: 05-12-13-22-25-35.

The New York Gaming Commission knew that the winning ticket was purchased at a New York City bodega, but they didn't know who bought the ticket. Winners have one year to step forward for the prize, and the day of reckoning was rapidly approaching.

Since the guys at the New York Lottery are nice enough, they began to spread the word. "We urge New York Lottery players: Check your pockets. Check your glove box. Look under the couch cushions. If you have this winning ticket, we look forward to meeting you," encouraged Gweneth Dean, director of the Commission's Division of the Lottery.

A retired security officer, Smith happened to catch a news report about the search for the lucky winner. He was suddenly inspired to look through his old tickets. He approached the closet where the old shirt waited. When he saw that the numbers were a perfect match, he "stood there for a minute thinking, 'Do I see what I think I see?'"

"I had to stick my head out the window and breathe in some fresh air," Smith claimed. "I was in serious doubt. I really had to convince myself this was real."

Despite his age, Smith decided to receive the payments over 26 long years. We're not questioning your decision, Jimmie. We'd only like to say: Enjoy your retirement!

CHAPTER 10:

TEEN'S UPLIFTING NOTES ON BRIDGE SAVE SIX LIVES

There's nothing like an inspiring or morale-boosting note from someone special to you to keep you moving in the right direction. One teen actually went a bit further: her uplifting notes written and tied to a British bridge in Sunderland helped save the precious lives of six people who thought they couldn't get through another day.

An example of one of Paige´s notes in 2018 was: "Even though things are difficult, your life matters; you're a shining light in a dark world, so just hold on." Northumbria Police Chief Superintendent Sarah Pitt claimed that Hunter´s approach was an "innovative way to reach out to those in a dark place."

Paige and the police both stressed how important it is to encourage people to speak out about their mental health struggles. Pitt added: "Paige has shown an incredible understanding of vulnerable people in need of support. For somebody so young, Paige has shown real maturity, and we thought it would only be right to thank her personally. She should be very proud of herself."

Paige had battled with her own mental health troubles, and in 2016, she began by attaching a few dozen notes to the bridge. Over time, she made it a personal point to add more hopeful notes, as many as she was able.

Not only was Paige´s initiative praised, but it was decided that Notes of Hope would be a lasting feature of the Wearmouth Bridge. This was thanks to a unanimous vote by local officials. "Every single suicide is a tragedy," Councilor Dominic McDonough declared.

"It's a bomb that destroys not just one life, but the lives of everyone who´s connected with the person who is lost. The most tragic thing is that suicide is preventable, and these lives can be saved," the councilor concluded.

Almost 240 handwritten signs were already in place on the bridge, and more were added in line with the community´s wishes. Paige admitted feeling "overwhelmed and thankful": her tireless work would now become a standing fixture on the bridge.

CHAPTER 11:

BUDWEISER MISSES SUPER BOWL: USES MARKETING MONEY FOR VACCINE AWARENESS INSTEAD

If you're an American football fan, you wouldn't miss the Super Bowl for the world, especially knowing that it's the biggest sporting event on the planet. But in 2021 one of the grandest advertisers in the history of the game decided to sit it out.

That's right: Budweiser, The King of Beers, stayed on the sidelines in 2021, for the first time in 37 long years, choosing instead to use the marketing money the company saved to spread information about the effectiveness of vaccines in fighting against that lousy sickness that comes from Covid-19.

In the week before Super Bowl LV (55, for those of us who weren't born in ancient Rome), Budweiser decided to run its Super Bowl ad on digital platforms. The commercial focused on the resilience of Americans during the coronavirus pandemic and included a select group of healthcare workers among the first to be jabbed with the vaccine. Actress Rashida Jones, popular for roles in *The Office* and *Parks and Recreation*, narrated the ad.

What did Alice Sylvester, co-founder of Sequent Partners, a marketing measurement and analytics company, have to say about Budweiser taking "its purpose-driven marketing to the next level"? She claimed the beer giant differentiated itself from other Super Bowl advertisers whose ads will air during the big game.

"It speaks to the long-tail impact of Super Bowl advertising, which is as much about brand building than it is about short-term revenue generation," Sylvester explained.

But the company isn't giving up completely on promoting its beer either. Bud agreed to give U.S. consumers (who were at least 21 years old) a free beer when they visited ABeerOnBud.com between January 25 and February 7, 2021. We´re still not totally sure if that was a virtual beer or a real one, but we assume it was the latter.

Iconic drink maker Coke also decided to miss the game, saying it has chosen to focus on "investing in the right resources," according to CNBC. The pandemic upended the beverage giant's business because fewer drinks were consumed outside people's homes. Coca-Cola's revenue dropped 13% during 2020's first nine months.

You might already know that running a short Super Bowl ad doesn't come cheap, especially with upward of 100 million fans tuning in. If you're thinking about running an ad, one 30-second commercial during the showcase game cost about $5.5 million in 2021, a tick lower than the $5.6 million total demanded in 2020.

CHAPTER 12:

CHINESE WOMAN HELPS 20 FAMILIES FIND MISSING KIDS, THEN FINDS HER OWN

Would you honestly be able to help other people find their missing kids first if yours was also missing? Surely, not many citizens would look out for others before their own families. Yet, when your son is kidnapped and goes missing for 32 years, you might not have a lot of hope that he'd eventually turn up either.

Mao Yin was just two years old when he vanished in Xian, the capital city in China´s Shaanxi province, in 1988. It turns out he was sold to another family who then raised him as their own.

Mao Yin was Jingzhi and her husband's only child, and China's one-child policy was then in full force, so there was no chance to have more. Naturally, she wanted her boy to study hard and be successful, so she nicknamed him ´Jia Janghi´ which means ´great´.

"Jia Jia was very well-behaved, smart, obedient, and a sensible child. He didn't like to cry. He was very lively and adorable. He was the kind of child that everyone liked when they saw him," Jingzhi recalls. She and her husband would drop him off at a nearby kindergarten in the morning and pick him up after work.

One day, when Jingzhi was traveling on business, she received alarming news from her company: her dear son was missing, and she should return home immediately. The dad had been in charge of the boy and left him alone for a minute to get water at a family hotel, only to find their treasure had disappeared in a flash.

The mother began to ask if anyone had seen Jia great. ´ in the area around the hotel. She ultimately printed 100,000 flyers with the boy´s picture and handed them out around Xian's train and bus stations. She also placed missing person announcements in local papers. Every effort she made met no success.

She had little idea about the spread of child abduction at the time in China - a direct result of the country's one-child policy. Parents who couldn't give birth to a boy were desperate to carry on the family name but afraid of the government's harsh penalties.

"My heart hurt. I wanted to cry. I wanted to scream," lamented Jingzhi. "I felt as though my heart had been emptied." At first, the wife blamed her husband, but then they began to work in earnest together to find the boy. But four years passed, with both parents more and more desperate, and they ultimately decided to divorce (and we promised you this is a book full of uplifting stories!).

Finally, Jingzhi checked into a hospital on the advice of a friend. She claims a doctor said something that truly impacted her: "I can treat you for your physical illnesses, but as for the illness in your heart, that's up to you."

Jingzhi became aware there were numerous parents whose children went missing - not just in Xian, but everywhere. She began to work with them, forming a network touching most Chinese provinces. They exchanged big bags of fliers with each other and posted them in the areas where they were responsible.

The network generated many more leads overall, though unfortunately, none brought Jia great. ´ any closer. All told, Jingzhi visited ten of China´s 31 provinces in her search. The marvelous mom began to work with an organization called Baby Come Home, helping 29 families reunite with their long, lost loved ones.

Jingzhi's mother passed away at age 94 in 2015, but before leaving this world, she informed her daughter that she'd dreamed Jia Janghi's would return. Wouldn't you know it: on Mother´s Day that year, the Chinese government contacted Jingzhi with the news that her son had been found, living some 435 miles away. Facial recognition and a DNA test confirmed the match.

Although the 32-year search resulted in a joyful reunion, son Jia Janghi's simply couldn't remember anything before the age of four. Yet, thanks to the Chinese government and the national media´s efforts to publicize the problem, the volume of child abduction cases has decreased.

There are still multiple families searching for their missing kids, as well as many grown children looking for their birth parents. All this means there's still much more work for Jingzhi to do. "I will continue to help people find their families," the mother calmly stated.

CHAPTER 13:

GIRL BULLIED FOR COLLECTING TRASH WINS GLOBAL AWARD

Nobody likes a bully, do they? This is especially true when the bully, or bullies as the case may be, pick on somebody for doing something that is helpful to everyone else. And maybe the most uplifting part of the whole story is that the girl who was bullied never stopped doing the helpful stuff (and she even won a global award, and lots of social media followers for it, to boot).

During the past few years, Nadia Sparkes's dedication to picking up garbage on her bike ride to school made headlines. A local paper in Norfolk, England, featured a story about her accomplishments, and how other kids at her school bullied her for those, calling her "Trash Girl" - a label that Nadia decided to proudly own.

The article went viral, which made the bullying tail off for a couple of months. But then the kids went at it again. Sadly, Nadia believed that her school didn't truly support her. She felt let down when the head teacher suggested that she lay off the litter-picking to appease the bullies.

Originally from Hellesdon, Nadia decided to leave her old school and its bullies behind. She transferred to Reepham High School, well known for being extremely eco-conscious. The youngster said she was "very excited about the move," and was thrilled about being part of the new school and continuing to spread her "Trash Girl" message.

Her next adventure took her to London where she picked up the 'Points of Light' award given by no less than the then Prime Minster, Theresa May.

CHAPTER 14:

HACKER FIXES PEOPLE'S ROUTERS SO THEY CAN'T BE HACKED BY OTHERS

Would you even know if your computer was being hacked? I certainly wouldn't, unless money started to disappear from my bank account, or some crazy hacker covered my screen with smiley faces or other emoticons (if that's what they're called).

Most of us also would think that a grey hat is a kind of boring, not-really-colorful cap that somebody chooses to wear. In this case, because we're touching on technology, let's find out about a Russian-speaking "grey-hat hacker" who finds weaknesses in regular people's routers that could be hacked into by the bad guys. Except, out of the goodness of his heart, he patches them - for free.

In general, the Russians haven´t gotten a very good rap recently, for obvious reasons. But there still exist some who help others, and for no charge. This specific hacker goes by the name of Alexey. He claims he works as a server administrator and says he's already disinfected over 100,000 MikroTik routers.

If you're like most people, you probably have no idea what kind of router you use. But you'd also be thrilled to know that a hacker (somebody normally considered a kind of crook) went into yours, without being asked, and fixed a gap or a hole or an entry that might allow other bad dudes to steal something from you, your family, or friends.

"I added firewall rules that blocked access to the router from outside the local network," admitted the adept Alexey. "In the comments, I wrote information about the vulnerability, and left the address of the @router_os Telegram channel, where they could ask questions."

Despite adjusting firewall settings to help over 100,000 users, Alexey claims that only 50 users reached out via Telegram. A few even said "thanks," but most were angry that somebody had done something to their routers without permission, even if it was meant to make their lives easier and more secure.

CHAPTER 15:

KIDS FINALLY GET A PERMIT FOR A LEMONADE STAND, THEN SELL OUT

You may know by now that once industrious kids have a particular plan in mind, there's not much you can do to stop them. After a picture of twins Kamari and Kamera's lemonade stand showed up online in 2020, some grinch actually dared to ask if the seven-year-olds had a permit (this is serious, folks) or not.

Think about it for a moment - mix the powder with water, get some cups, set up a streetside table, and create a paper sign with crayons - no, completing permit papers was definitely not on the twins' lemonade stand To-Do list. Fortunately, this detour in the road wasn't a match for the undeniable spirit of two sisters with a scheme (especially one involving money, and potentially a lot of it - especially if the weather stays hot).

Kamari and Kamera of Savannah, Georgia, weren't about to let the golden opportunity slip through their grasp. The girls refused to stop selling their "twin-monade," as they refer to it. In fact, they readily filled out the forms needed, and actually got themselves a lemonade stand permit (assuming that's what it's called since we´re not exactly lawyers).

Once they reopened, the twins were inundated with community support. There was a constant long line to purchase one of the multiple flavors of ice-cold lemonade the girls had to offer. In fact, on Juneteenth, there was a wait of an hour to buy a glass of "twin-monade."

Quite literally, there was a line around the block to sponsor these two mini-entrepreneurs. At the end of the day, the girls even made enough money from their booming lemonade sales to buy themselves a pair of fancy phones - with permit in hand.

CHAPTER 16:

FINLAND OFFERS NEW DADS AS MUCH PAID LEAVE AS MOMS

Besides being the reported home of Santa Claus, Finland also treats its new dads pretty well. In fact, Finland's new government announced its 2020 plans to give all parents the same amount of maternity and paternity leave, in an attempt to persuade fathers to spend more time with their kids, from the start.

This paid allowance would increase to a combined 14 months, which works out to a whopping 164 days per parent. Neighboring Sweden has Europe's most generous parental leave system with 240 days for each mom and dad after a baby's birth. Finland claims that it wants to "promote well-being and gender equality."

Aino-Kaisa Pekonen, the Finnish health and social affairs minister, told reporters that "a radical reform of family benefits" had started, with the express goal of making parental relationships stronger from Day 1, literally speaking.

On average in Finland, only one in four dads take what they´re allowed. The new plans guarantee that each parent receives 6.6 months of leave (164 days under Finland's six-day-week benefit system), and pregnant women will now receive an extra month's allowance.

"Norway was the first country in 1993 to have non-transferable leave for fathers and then Sweden followed suit. But Denmark instituted a father quota in 1998 and abolished it later, and it hasn't been re-introduced," Ms. Pekonen explained. Does it seem like Santa might actually work undercover for the government in Finland?

CHAPTER 17:

FARMER STUDIES LAW FOR 16 YEARS AND BEATS POLLUTERS

Here's another guy studying law around the clock to beat back the bad guys. In this case, it's a farmer who hit the books for a full 16 years, in the middle of his yeoman efforts in the fields, to get a leg up on the chemical company responsible for polluting his land.

Wang Enlin, a Chinese man who boasted only three years of formal education, still won the first round in a high-profile case against the government-owned Qihua Group, according to the *People's Daily Online*.

Even though the Qihua Group, whose assets are estimated at a neat two billion yuan (or $265 million), has fought the decision, the elderly gentleman vowed that he's determined to win justice for his neighbors and himself since they couldn't grow healthy crops on their tainted land anymore.

Mr. Wang is in his sixties, and lives in the village of Yushutun just outside Qiqihar in Heilongjiang Province described by *People's Daily Online*, which also cited *China Youth Daily*. Wang said he'd never forget the year 2001 when his land was flooded by toxic waste released by the Qihua Group.

It's hard to imagine, but on the eve of the Lunar New Year, Mr. Wang was enjoying a game of cards with neighbors while making dumplings. Suddenly, the house they were in was flooded by wastewater from the Qihua factory around the corner.

More critically, the wastewater also covered part of the village's precious farmland that the residents depended on to make a living. In 2001, Wang wrote a letter to the Qiqihar's Land Resources Bureau to demand action for the pollution Qihua had introduced to his village.

While dealing with the local officials, he was repeatedly asked to produce evidence showing that the village's land had been ruined. Wang claimed, "I knew I was in the right, but I didn't know what law the other party had broken, or whether or not there was evidence." He gave the interview in his tiny home, which cost 50 yuan ($6.60) per month to rent from the village authorities.

The farmer dropped out of school in the third grade but began reading through dozens of law books with the help of a dictionary. At the time, he simply didn't have the money to buy the books, so he spent weeks on end reading the books at the local bookstore and copying the relevant information by hand. In return, Wang would give free bags of corn to the shopkeeper for allowing him to stay.

After an incredible 16 years of putting his nose to the grindstone, Wang gladly used the legal know-how he'd acquired to help his neighbors gather proof of pollution with which to confront the Qihua Group.

CHAPTER 18:

GHANAIAN TEACHER TAUGHT MS WORD ON BOARD, GETS COMPUTER DONATIONS

Obviously, there are some things we can learn on the trusty chalkboard (maybe nowadays it's a whiteboard or glass panel). But the old saying goes: "You learn by doing." There's no better example than using cell phones or computers. You've really got to get your fingers on the devices to figure out how to make them go.

But a Ghanaian teacher named Richard Appiah Akoto didn't have any computer to teach his students, or any resources to plan ahead either. Yet he still used his drawing talent, enthusiasm, and expertise to explain in detail to his students the ins and outs of Microsoft Word, and in the process, gained worldwide admiration and headlines.

Richard Appiah Akoto became an overnight sensation for teaching computer tech without a computer on hand at Betenase M/A Junior High School in the town of Sekyedumase in South Ghana. He's begun to reap the fruits of this unexpected media attention.

Prominent people and organizations have been donating desktop and laptop computers to Akoto's school. In addition, as part of Microsoft's vow to offer him free training, Akoto was jetted to faraway Singapore to attend the yearly Microsoft Educators Exchange.

After coming across the Facebook post that took Akoto to the world, a Saudi philanthropist at the UK's University of Leeds sent him a laptop "as a small gift to his students," he said. "I always understand from the teachings of Islam that useful knowledge is crucial for the benefit of the self and humanity," Amirah Alharthi, a PhD student in the statistics department at Leeds, informed CNN.

Alharthi's gift wasn't the last. Motivated by the teacher's story, NIIT Ghana, a computer training school located in the capital of Accra, sent five desktop computers to the school, along with books and a special laptop for Akoto. The center manager at NIIT, Ashish Kumar, said he'd seen snapshots of the beaming teacher going viral on Facebook and CNN, along with other media organizations.

CHAPTER 19:

RAPPER DECLARES $1 MILLION DONATION TO CHICAGO PUBLIC SCHOOLS

Whether you like rap music or not, you've got to appreciate the benevolence of a Chicago rapper called Chance who decided to donate $1 million to the Chicago public school district.

"Our kids should not be held hostage because of political positions," Chance declared. The announcement followed his meeting with Bruce Rauner, Illinois governor, in which they went back and forth about public education and other "important issues" affecting the city of Chicago, and the state of Illinois as a whole.

Right after the meeting, Chance vented his frustration: "It went a little different than it should have." The rapper claimed he was given empty answers during his encounter with the governor. At a press conference later, he repeated that Rauner provided him with "vague" answers, and shouted, "Gov. Rauner, do your job!"

Well, we've all wanted to shout at our governor at one point or another, especially if we thought he or she'd actually listen to us (based on the fact that we might donate oodles of money to our state's public schools).

The three-time Grammy award-winning superstar's real name is Chancelor Bennet, and he's a proud product of the Chicago Public Schools. A native of the Chatham neighborhood. Chance's public mission started on March 6, 2017 when he pledged $1 million of his own money to the Chicago Public School Foundation. He also held a separate Teacher Appreciation event.

The very same day, he requested that private businesses and corporations also donate money to the school system, promising that for every $100,000 in donations that roll in, he'll give an additional $10,000 to individual schools to further support arts education. What are "the chances" that some Chicago-area students who love the arts will continue to thrive?

CHAPTER 20:

PERRY PAYS ALL
SENIOR-HOUR GROCERIES

What would you say if you finally got to the supermarket cashier with hundreds of dollars' worth of groceries, and some kind gent stepped up at that very moment and offered to foot the bill?

"Senior and higher-risk Kroger shoppers in Metro Atlanta did receive a nice surprise at the register this morning when they learned Tyler Perry had paid their grocery tab in full," reported Felix Turner, Atlanta spokesperson for Kroger.

"We'd like to join our customers in thanking Mr. Perry for his kindness and generosity during this unprecedented pandemic. It was truly a pleasure to see our customers filled with joy and gratitude as the news spread throughout 44 stores across metro Atlanta," Turner concluded.

Back in April of 2020, Atlanta media mogul Tyler Perry took care of the grocery bills for all shoppers during the so-called Senior Hour at a grand total of 44 Kroger supermarkets in Metro Atlanta, as well as at 29 Winn-Dixies in his hometown of New Orleans. That's a pretty penny indeed.

Phil Kloer (64) remembered going to a Decatur Kroger during the Senior Hour and was nearly finished with his shopping when an employee approached him and quietly told him to make sure to get to the cashier by 8 a.m.

"I was almost done shopping, so that wasn't a big deal," he recalled. When he did arrive, he saw a Kroger grocery bag covering the credit card reader and was ready to take it off when the cashier told him that he shouldn't worry. She then told him Perry had his $290 in groceries "under control."

"I was dumbstruck," Kloer, previously a reporter at *The Atlanta Journal Constitution*, admitted. We must confess, that guy Perry seems pretty cool to us.

CHAPTER 21:

BILLIONAIRE LAUNCHES DRUG COMPANY DEDICATED TO LOW-COST GENERICS AND TRANSPARENCY

We know you'd probably like to save on groceries, but what about medications? They tend to run even higher. In January 2022, the Mark Cuban Cost Plus Drug Company (MCCPDC) launched its pharmacy online as part of a continuous drive to provide consumers with low prices for drugs and medications.

Cuban's pharmacy says it offers considerable savings, with several prescription meds coming in at more than half the cost of the next best option in terms of price. For example, the leukemia treatment 'Imatinib' has a hefty retail price of $9,657 a month, according to MCCPDC, in comparison to $120 with a common voucher. Yet the price through the new online pharmacy is a mere $47 per month.

The pharmacy's initial inventory at launch is comprised of 100 generic drugs. MCCDPC's plan is to skip the so-called middleman, as well as markups, and claims that its prices reflect those of actual manufacturers, along with a flat 15% fee.

Also, to move away from working with pharmacy benefit managers, the pharmacy will work with cash only. The virtual pharmacy runs on Truepill's digital health platform and depends on its profile as a national pharmacy to fill and deliver prescriptions.

"We will do whatever it takes to get affordable pharmaceuticals to patients," declared Alex Oshmyansky, CEO of Mark Cuban Cost Plus Drug, in a prepared statement. "The markup on potentially lifesaving drugs that people depend on is a problem that can't be ignored. It's imperative that we take action and help expand access to these medications for those who need them most."

Mark Cuban is the owner of the NBA's Dallas Mavericks, and he appears to be a maverick in getting low-cost meds to needy patients at the same time.

CHAPTER 22:

JETBLUE CAPS FLIGHTS AT $99, HELPS CITIZENS ESCAPE HURRICANE

If you've ever been in or around a raging hurricane, you know it's not a lot of fun. Thus, you'd be pleased to hear the news on JetBlue, the airline that capped its flight prices at just below a hundred bucks a pop (including government taxes!) to help individuals escape Florida and the wrath of onrushing Hurricane Irma in 2017. Several other carriers, like American and Delta, went along with the program.

For previous reservations, JetBlue also waived cancellation fees, change fees, and airfare differences when rebooking. "Given that many Floridians are struggling to get out of harm's way, this is welcome news," Bill Nelson, a Democratic Senator from Florida, said in an emailed statement sent by a spokesperson. "I hope more airlines do the right thing and follow suit."

Delta went a step further, drumming up extra flights during the time of need. "We're also adding flights, and increasing the size of the aircraft we're using on flights to and from San Juan and South Florida, providing more opportunities for customers to leave. New flights are being added to and from San Juan, Miami, Palm Beach, Fort Lauderdale, and Key West, all to Atlanta (where people can connect to destinations across the U.S.)," a Delta representative informed the public.

A number of travelers spoke out about steep prices as they hustled to book tickets to hightail it away from the storm. Some even mentioned prices above $1,000. American, Delta, and JetBlue came to the rescue!

CHAPTER 23:

THE COST OF INSULIN
CAPPED AT $35 BY HOUSE

The House approved a bill limiting the cost of insulin to no more than $35 a month in a decision that would positively impact diabetics across the U.S. "There's no time off when you live with diabetes," affirmed Lucy McBath, a Democratic representative from Georgia. She, Rep. Daniel Kildee (D-MI), and Rep. Joseph Morelle (D-NY) were responsible for co-sponsoring the Affordable Insulin Now Act in the House.

McBath continued with a compelling question, "Why is it that a child born with this disease must spend around $6,000 a year for life on a drug that has been around for over a century?" Supporters of the bill claimed it would help prevent diabetics from needing to choose between buying life-saving medicine and paying the bills.

"Americans are paying more than ten times the price of insulin as people in other high-income countries," Representative Frank Pallone, Jr. (D-NJ) declared. On the other hand, opponents countered that the government shouldn't be put in the position of dictating prices to the private sector.

Nevertheless, Shaheen and Collins asserted in a joint statement: "Access to insulin is a matter of life or death for many people living with diabetes. Cost should never be a barrier for those whose lives literally depend on affording this medication.

"Negotiations are ongoing, but there's a bipartisan determination to present policy proposals that both cap out-of-pocket costs, and address soaring insulin prices that for too long have forced some Americans to ration their supplies. That's unacceptable, and it's time we put an end to it," the two concluded.

CHAPTER 24:

PAKISTAN TO PLANT BILLIONS OF TREES USING THOUSANDS OF UNEMPLOYED WORKERS

Construction worker Abdul Rahman lost his job because of Pakistan's coronavirus lockdown. At that moment, his options were severely limited: turn to begging on the streets, or let his dear family go hungry.

But the Pakistani government offered him a better choice: Join thousands of other unemployed workers in a tree-planting action all across the country to deal with the increasing threat of climate change.

Out-of-work day laborers were given new jobs as "jungle workers," responsible for planting saplings as part of the nation's '10 Billion Tree Tsunami' program. This kind of "green stimulus" effort is one example of how funds marked to help families and keep the economy running during the pandemic shutdown could also help countries get ready for the next big challenge: climate change.

"Due to the coronavirus, all the cities have shut down, and there is no work. Most of us daily wagers couldn't earn a living," Rahman, who resides in the Rawalpindi district of Punjab province, informed the Thomson Reuters Foundation. He could make 500 rupees (around $3) a day planting trees - half of what he might have otherwise earned on a good day previously, but enough to squeeze by.

"All of us now have a way of earning daily wages again to feed our families," Rahman said. The ambitious five-year tree-planting scheme, launched in 2018 by Prime Minister Imran Khan, seeks to fight back against increasing temperatures, flooding, droughts, and other extreme weather conditions that specialists are linking to the specter of climate change.

CHAPTER 25:

POLICE DOG FIRED FOR FRIENDLINESS, NOW HAS A NEW JOB AS A GREETER

We'd like to share the latest uplifting news from a website called *Bored Panda*: It's time for you to meet Gavel, the German shepherd that was fired from his job as a police dog for actually being too nice for this line of work.

That's right: rather than sniffing out bombs and catching robbers for the Queensland Police Service in Brisbane, Australia, the adorable puppy seemed keen on getting a belly rub or a back scratch.

However, given the fact that he's a good-looking service dog, he didn't need to spend a lot of time standing in the unemployment line. He quickly secured an even better position for himself. All he had to do was be his normal sociable and charming self to become the official "Vice-Regal Working Dog."

When Governor Paul de Jersey first encountered police officer Gavel, he was only a 10-week-old puppy. The canine in question was due to live at the governor's official residence during his training. At the precise moment that the politician heard the lovely dog's training was off because of his excessive friendliness, he jumped in and officially adopted the pup.

Finally, Gavel got to sign (or paw?) the contract stipulating his duties, including extending a warm welcome to special visitors, and going along to official ceremonies, often all dressed up in fancy clothes. Gavel, you've already done quite well for yourself, without a whole lot of expensive training!

CHAPTER 26:

TEXAS INVESTOR USES GAINS TO HELP SICK KIDS

Back in January of 2021, there was plenty of drama on Wall Street related to some companies called GameStop and Robinhood. At the same time, several investors participating in the "short sale" of GameStop decided to turn their proceeds toward doing good deeds for others.

One specific investor, desiring anonymity, took 10 Nintendo switches purchased at various GameStop locations in the Dallas-Fort Worth area to Medical City Children's Hospital. The investor said his actions were possible because of his gains on GME.

A group of small investors carried out a campaign to challenge big hedge funds by pushing up the share price of several ailing retailers and GameStop, based in a place called Grapevine.

The campaign kicked off on Reddit and other online discussion platforms, where small investors spurred each other into buying GameStop stock, making much bigger players such as hedge funds attempt to cover their bets by buying the stock, as a result increasing the price even more.

The anonymous and generous investor who donated the Nintendo Switch game players said they'd earned "a good amount through 'r/WallStreetBets' on this hilarious GME trade" and was inspired to return the favor "in a way that was equally hilarious."

The investor hoped to get others from the Reddit forum 'r/WallStreetBets' to give back in kind and turn the GameStop short sale into "a force for good." And if you ever see kids cutting loose on a Nintendo Switch game player, you know that it can be hilarious, as well as quite noisy.

CHAPTER 27:

DAMAGE TO NOTRE DAME CATHEDRAL NOT AS BAD AS WE THOUGHT

On April 15, 2019, a tragic fire destroyed many priceless artifacts inside France's Notre Dame Cathedral. It took 23 minutes for the blaze to be found after alarms had already sounded a dire warning. But a heroic team stormed into the fiery 850-year-old cathedral to save the religious icon from destruction.

As gigantic flames leapt around the church, and cascades of sparks illuminated the night sky of Paris, the rescue team charged fearlessly into the raging inferno. Firefighters continued to battle the blaze for eight hours, even though the cathedral's roof and spire were eventually lost.

However, despite worries that the entire building would collapse, somehow the stone structure and symbolic bell towers continue to stand as we speak. Thanks to the brave actions of the firefighters, and their quick decision to use a robot to hose down the cathedral, invaluable treasures dating back to ancient times, including antiquities said to be linked to the Crucifixion, together with stained-glass creations from the 13th century, could withstand the scorching flames.

In particular, the three "irreplaceable" Rose Windows (each almost a thousand years old) that were feared to have either melted or exploded, were miraculously discovered intact. Luckily, most of the cathedral's major religious objects and exquisite works of art - including The Crown of Thorns, a tunic worn by King Louis IX, and copper sculptures of 16 Biblical figures - escaped serious harm.

Paris's Deputy Mayor for Tourism and Sports, Jean-Francois Martins, said that individual bystanders rapidly created a human chain to salvage many precious relics stored inside the cathedral as quickly as possible. Furthermore, the chaplain of the Paris Fire Department, Father Jean-Marc Fournier, made it his mission to save the consecrated hosts that Catholics believe represent the body and blood of Christ.

CHAPTER 28:

DENVER HIRES HOMELESS; NOW 100 HAVE NEW JOBS

Jeffrey Maes wasn't ever expecting to have to live on the street when he reached his fifties. He'd been brave enough to start various businesses, but unfortunately, the final one, a remodeling company, went belly up just as he was stretched to the limit on four different properties. He ended up losing them all and wound up without a home for himself - along with the understanding that he was termed "unemployable" by the market.

However, in 2017, he found out about a day-labor scheme sponsored by the Mile High City that had helped other friends battle back to their feet. After almost four years of living hand to mouth on the mean streets, Maes decided to give it a go.

Eventually, he spoke about how the Denver Day Works program helped to rejuvenate his flagging pride, as well as helping him find a full-time job. He got into retrofitting lights at the Central Library when city officials announced the program's expansion the following year.

During a news conference, Mayor Michael Hancock and others reported that the first-year numbers went well beyond the majority of their goals. One year after the program's launch in November of 2016, Denver Human Services said that 284 people worked at least a day - with all but 10 sticking around longer - carrying out landscaping duties in parks, assisting in the Denver Elections Division, and helping public-works crews, among other job activities.

Among those participants, Maes was one of 110 who secured full-time work, with 15 scoring permanent or project-based city jobs, while the rest managed to find work with dozens of external private and public employers.

"When you take a good person who is down, broken, discouraged, and you give them an opportunity to be proud of themselves - to stand up and do something for themselves - that's one of the greatest gifts anybody can give to anybody," Maes, 57, stressed. "And for that, I'd like to say thank you." The city of Denver thanks you, Mr. Maes.

CHAPTER 29:

CELEB CENA HAS GRANTED 800 MAKE-A-WISH REQUESTS

This character came all the way from being a skinny kid, who was targeted by bullies, to a record-setting World Wrestling Entertainment (WWE) champion, and leading movie man. After checking out his trajectory, it certainly looks like the sky's the limit for John Cena (well, his head doesn't exactly scratch the sky at 6'1", but his physique definitely turns heads here on earth).

In addition to all the trophies, Cena now adds the title of generous "wish-granter" to his resumé. First as a wrestler, and later as an actor, John has helped more than 600 kids realize their dreams through his volunteer work on behalf of Make-A-Wish, a non-profit gig that focuses on granting life-altering wishes to youngsters battling severe conditions and illnesses.

This total number of wishes granted appears even more incredible when we find out that Cena stumbled upon the organization unintentionally in 2002 while he was a WWE rookie. "My first Make-A-Wish, I was kind of shuffled - it wasn't for me, I think the person wanted to meet another superstar," Cena admitted. "But the WWE does a great job of like, "Hey, there's a Make-A-Wish kid in this room. Can you come to say hello?" So, a bunch of people are shuttled in to say hello to a young fan of WWE.

"So, we're shuttled in, and I said my hellos and took my pictures and then left. And they're like, 'Thank you, Make-A-Wish thanks you.' I was like, 'What is Make-A-Wish?'" recalled Cena.

However, as soon as the *Trainwreck* sensation learned what the foundation really stood for, he went all out to give charity work priority over all else going on in his whirlwind life. "I said, 'If you ever need me for this, I don't care what I'm doing, I will drop what I'm doing and be involved because I think that's the coolest thing,'" Cena elaborated.

"We've all experienced that joy of giving a gift for the holidays where you just nail it -

that's the same gift I get in giving back to people's lives, in being able to give them wonderful emotional moments," the WWE maestro explained.

What's more, in December of 2018, the grappler and Hailee Steinfeld teamed up with the Make-A-Wish guys to transform the Empire State Building into a giant glowing structure in honor of their movie *Bumblebee*. This was simply in addition to his dedication to brightening up kids' lives.

Whether pro wrestling is fake or not, the uplifting effect of Make-A-Wish on needy kids is definitely not.

CHAPTER 30:

FIRST BLACK FEMALE CONFIRMED TO SUPREME COURT

2022 was a historic year for various reasons. A big one was when the Senate voted to confirm Judge Ketanji Brown Jackson to the Supreme Court, guaranteeing her place in history as the first Black woman to participate in the USA's highest court.

Jackson's confirmation as the 116th justice in American history received bipartisan support, with a final vote of 53 to 47 in the upper chamber. Three Republicans - Senators Susan Collins of Maine, Lisa Murkowski of Alaska, and Mitt Romney of Utah - went along with all 50 Democrats in supporting President Biden's nominee.

Vice President Kamala Harris, the first female and first woman of color to serve in that role, conducted the Senate during the unprecedented decision.

"On this vote, the 'yays' are 53. The nays are 47, and this nomination is confirmed," Harris declared proudly to a round of rousing applause from the senators.

Jackson's appointment to the high court should be a significant part of President Biden's legacy and was his first opportunity to make his mark on the Supreme Court. Yet Jackson didn't take the bench immediately, as Justice Stephen Breyer, whose seat she would fill, was set to retire at the end of the Supreme Court's summer.

President Biden commemorated the historic vote together with Jackson in the White House's Roosevelt Room. Photographers snapped the two hugging as the Senate passed the magic number needed for her confirmation.

"This is a wonderful day, a joyous day, an inspiring day for the Senate, for the Supreme Court, and for the United States of America," Senate Majority Leader Chuck Schumer proclaimed just prior to the vote. "Today is one of the brightest lights, and let us hope it's a metaphor - an indication of many more bright lights to come."

CHAPTER 31:

MALI GIVES ELEPHANTS A FIGHTING CHANCE

The African country of Mali indeed has elephants, but they're just one of two remaining desert herds in the world and could be gone in a mere three years if the government doesn't do more to protect them, a conservation group has warned.

Poachers have taken advantage of the chaos from a growing Islamist insurgency and other unrest in the country's lawless north to step up ivory trafficking - a trade that the United Nations says bankrolls those militants.

Sixteen elephants were killed in January 2016, adding to more than 80 slaughtered in 2015, said Susan Canney, director of the Mali Elephant Project for the WILD Foundation. "We have 50 rangers waiting to be deployed, but they're held up waiting for official approval and firearms from the government," Canney informed Reuters.

"Mali is standing by, while the elephants are being slaughtered. If we continue at this rate, they'll all be gone in three years." The last aerial census in 2007 showed 350 animals. The African deserts and savannahs stretching between the Gulf of Guinea and the Nile Basin once possessed tens of thousands of elephants, but illegal hunting and loss of habitat drastically cut their numbers.

Most now live in small, scattered groups. Namibia is home to the world's only other known desert herd. Yet the Tuareg nomads who share the elephants' territory "have a remarkable culture of toleration," biologist Iain Douglas-Hamilton says, and they don't hunt the animals.

There's also "great political will in Mali to protect these animals and perhaps see them as a mobile national park." Malians already demonstrated their affection when a massive drought dried up the last remaining water source for the elephants in 1983, and the government (a constitutional democracy) trucked in water for the beasts.

In the end, nobody's quite sure if Mali's desert elephants really can be saved. But it's abundantly clear that local people value Mali's elephants for many reasons, most importantly because "if elephants disappear it means the environment is no longer good for us," one concerned Malian concluded.

CHAPTER 32:

INDIAN COUPLE BUYS LAND FOR TIGERS TO ROAM

His intense love of nature and wildlife led Aditya Singh to give up his comfortable job as an Indian civil servant in 1998, abandon his cozy house in Delhi, and move to a remote outpost in Rajasthan, on the border of the renowned Ranthambore Tiger Reserve in India. During the last two decades, Singh has kept busy buying up pieces of land next to Ranthambore and permitting the forest to return.

After moving to Sawai Madhopur, a smaller city close to the Ranthambore Tiger Reserve (RTR), Singh picked up photography as a hobby. He and his wife Poonam Singh also opened a resort for tourists but different from many resorts that push for unrestricted access to areas containing wildlife, they painstakingly bought plots of land as close to the RTR bounds as they could to allow the wild animals "more privacy."

"The area is called Bhadlav. I had first gone to this area soon after settling in Ranthambore along with a BBC filmmaker. This area, adjacent to the boundary of the Ranthambore Reserve, was visited by predators like tigers, who used to come for prey. As a result, farmers were selling their land," Singh recalled.

For her, Poonam claims it was love at first sight when she initially went to Ranthambore with Aditya. "My first sighting was a tigress with three cubs on a hill. It was magical. At the end of the trip, I just asked him if we could move to Ranthambore. He wanted it too, and within months we moved. As far as this land is concerned, it was a dream that we both saw and achieved together to have our own area of wilderness," she recalled fondly.

An artist by profession, Poonam managed the resort with Aditya for two decades until deciding to close up shop in 2019. Nowadays, they own around 35 acres of land in Bhadlav and another five-acre lot just hundreds of yards away, with a strip of land joining the two.

Their acreage has developed into a rich green tapestry visited by all sorts of wildlife, including tigers, leopards, and wild boars. Since then, the natural pressure of massive predators (like those very big cats with distinct orange and black stripes, and a bunch of sharp teeth, from RTR) wandering into farmers' fields has decreased considerably.

"It's simply because the animals understand that in this patch of forest, they get prey, water, and safe shelter without any disturbance," said Singh with a laugh.

CHAPTER 33:

DICAPRIO RAISES $100 MILLION TO FIGHT CLIMATE CHANGE

You might feel like your fighting days are behind you (they never are!), but Leonardo DiCaprio, at least, seems like he's only just getting started. The *Titanic* actor, who founded the Leonardo DiCaprio Foundation to increase awareness about climate change, wrote in a statement: "When I founded LDF 20 years ago, I did so based on the simple idea that we could make a real difference by directly funding some of the most effective environmental projects.

"Whether it be individuals, grassroots movements, or major nonprofits, we wanted to focus on getting critical funding to those who could have the greatest impact. We're extremely proud to celebrate 20 years of this model. Since 1998, we've supported over 200 projects on every continent and in every ocean, from habitat and species conservation, renewable energy, climate change, indigenous rights, and more."

It's safe to say Leo's had his fair share of trouble with awards (we don't really want to mention the Oscar saga), and his track record for environmental awards isn't much better. He was roundly criticized for heading off on a private jet to accept one in 2016.

DiCaprio's rep quickly explained to *US Weekly*: "He was asked to speak at both the Riverkeeper and amfAR events, but the only way to attend the two fundraisers was to hitch a ride with flights that were already planned. Leo helped both events raise millions, donated his own funds, auctioned off his house, and had speaking roles in both programs." Well, that makes Leo's behavior sound a bit better.

Even though DiCaprio is no stranger to criticism, he turned the focus back to the fight he's fighting (along with many of us): "Climate change is real. It is happening right now. It's the most urgent threat facing our entire species. We need to work together to stop procrastinating... Let us not take this planet for granted. I do not take tonight for granted," the famed actor stated.

CHAPTER 34:

SCHOOL SUPER HELPS A STUDENT WITH OWN INSURANCE – GETS SMALL FINE, BUT KEEPS JOB

An Indiana school superintendent was arrested and faced fraud charges for allegedly using her own son's name to help a sick student get proper medical treatment. Casey Smitherman, the Elwood Community School Corporation superintendent, was accused of insurance fraud, identity deception, insurance application fraud, and official misconduct, according to court documents. Wow, this doesn't really sound like the most uplifting story ever!

Elwood police in Indiana reported that they received a tip about Smitherman taking a 15-year-old student to urgent care on January 9, 2019, after the teen didn't show up at school because he had a sore throat, read a probable cause affidavit.

NBC News found out from Madison County Prosecutor Rodney Cummings that Smitherman accompanied the student to one urgent care location but was turned down because she wasn't the boy's legal guardian. Then Smitherman delivered the student to St. Vincent Med in Elwood where she used her own insurance to get the student checked under her son's name, Cummings continued.

In her defense, Smitherman informed police that she was concerned about the student when he didn't turn up at school. She dropped by his house and found that he was sick, in the words of the affidavit. After leaving urgent care, she stopped at a CVS Pharmacy to have an Amoxicillin prescription filled, once more using her insurance and son's name.

Why didn't Smitherman contact child welfare authorities about the boy's case? She worried that the student would be placed in a foster home. The superintendent said that she'd helped the student in the past, buying clothes for him and cleaning his home, stated the affidavit.

Finally, Smitherman was arrested and needed to pay $500 in bail to walk free. Elwood Community School Corporation released a statement declaring that Smitherman had made an "unfortunate mistake," but she still had their backing.

"We understand that it was out of concern for this child's welfare. We know she understands what she did was wrong, but she continues to have our support," the district reinforced to *The Herald Bulletin*.

CHAPTER 35:

CALIFORNIA FIRST STATE TO OFFER ALL STUDENTS FREE BREAKFAST AND LUNCH

Have you ever heard that there's no such thing as a free lunch? Well, that grand and very golden state of California has become the first in the nation to offer both breakfast and lunch for free to all its smiling students. And if you had California's budget, you'd probably be a bit happier too!

"We have a responsible, fiscally prudent budget. We responded to the public. We go after the problems that have been intractable for so long and budget for impact," stated Senator John Laird, D-Santa Cruz, who happened to have served in the Assembly during the Great Recession. That was when the legislature had to cope with huge cuts in state revenue.

"We've been waiting for decades to have student aid that helps people. We've been waiting to restore our schools financially. I don't think anybody has had a budget like this in front of them for a generation, if not longer. We should be proud of this budget," Laird concluded.

The budget year began July 1, 2021, and promised to significantly improve childcare, adding "universal transitional kindergarten" for four-year-old children during the next five years, and ensuring the country's first free breakfast and lunch for all students, starting in 2022-23.

In terms of higher education, the budget added $173 million in continuing funding for the University of California, $186 million for California State University, and $371 million for community colleges. It eliminated the Cal Grant age cutoff while increasing the Middle-Class Scholarship program to cover total attendance costs for lower- and middle-class UC and CSU students starting in 2022-23. If you're a fan of education, things were hunky dory in California.

As if all that wasn't enough, billions of dollars were rolled over as one-off funding to relieve the pandemic's impact on the mental health of students, and the setbacks they suffered in learning. It was also enough to pay off $11 billion in late payments that many of the state's districts accepted that year (called deferrals).

Now, why is it that I can't even balance my own checkbook?

CHAPTER 36:

BROOKLYN LANDLORD CANCELS RENT FOR HUNDREDS DURING COVID

In April 2020, Mario Salerno, a well-known landlord in Brooklyn, NY, said he didn't want renters in his buildings to get too stressed about their payments during the coronavirus pandemic.

Salerno, 59 years old, inherited the gas station that belonged to his dad on Metropolitan Avenue in the heart of the Brooklyn neighborhood of Williamsburg. But rather than spend the rest of his life pumping gas, Salerno invested shrewdly, and unit by unit accumulated 80 apartments along with 200 tenants in Brooklyn's Greenpoint and Williamsburg.

So, at the end of March that year, Salerno decided to pass on some of the good fortune he'd had over the years. He posted an uplifting notice on the front doors of each one of his units stating that rent would be waived for April.

"Due to the recent pandemic of Covid-19 affecting all of us, please note I am waiving rent for the month of April," declared the notice. Of course, as we all know, the Covid pandemic hit us hard for much more than a month. But every little bit helps.

One of the main reasons Mario said he'd waive rent for a month was that he hoped his tenants would be able to "worry about your neighbor, and worry about your family."

Salerno explained that he made the decision after listening to numerous tenants who were struggling to make ends meet because of the nasty virus. "I want everybody to be healthy," he claimed. "That's the whole thing."

Now you know: If you're ever facing similar trials and tribulations paying some kind of loan, or your rent, be nice and ask for help. There's no guarantee that every loan officer or landlord will look down on you as kindly as the sweet Salerno, but it's worth a try.

CHAPTER 37:

FIRST HYDROGEN-POWERED TRAINS RUN IN GERMANY, WITH ONLY EMISSIONS - CONDENSED WATER

Remember back in the old days of diesel fuel, when outdated cars and trains came rolling along, belching out all kinds of noxious fumes and smoke? At the moment in Germany, there's a sparkling new train service, fueled by hydrogen, and the only emissions end up being condensed water and some steam.

These trains don't pollute like they used to, and they're also super-quiet. The train's maker, Alstom, says that the Coradia iLint has a range of almost 625 miles. That means it can basically operate all day on the rails using a solitary tank of hydrogen. A filling station for hydrogen was established on the train route between Cuxhaven, Bremerhaven, Bremervörde, and Buxtehude.

You don't necessarily need to memorize these station names, but a clean, quiet trip thereabouts seems like a nice option. Despite efforts to electrify trains in many countries, a large part of Europe's rail network will continue to depend on trains that aren't electrified over the long haul. Even today, there are still more than 4,000 diesel-powered cars in Germany alone.

Switching the entire European continent to green energy is still a way off, but introducing such a sleek, hydrogen-powered train is surely a step in the right direction.

CHAPTER 38:

EVERY PORSCHE EMPLOYEE, EVEN CLEANING STAFF, RECEIVES A BONUS IN THE BEST YEAR EVER

Like most of us, you may be tired of hearing how top executives around the world continue to rake in outrageous bonuses, while hard-working middle management and factory workers still make relative peanuts.

On the other hand, every employee, including assembly line workers and janitors, at Porsche received a sweet 9,111-Euro ($9,825) bonus in 2017, the car company announced in a press release. The bonus is a result of the 911 (and not the emergency telephone number!), Porsche's jaw-dropping sports car that's been in non-stop production since 1963.

Porsche ramped up its deliveries to 237,778 vehicles in the 2016 business year, raising its revenue to 22.3 billion Euros ($24 billion). The German company's record year was mostly because of hot sales of crossover Sports Utility Vehicles (SUVs).

"In the end, no one in our large VW family received anywhere near as large a bonus as our employees at Porsche," wrote Uwe Hück, the chair of Porsche's Group Works Council. "We had to walk a very fine line during the negotiations. The result was this extraordinary and one-off, but completely justified, bonus."

But all you Porsche workers beware - if we read between the lines of the chairman's statement, we might imagine that this type of generous bonus won't happen again (the key term he used was "one-off"). Remember that money doesn't usually grow on trees.

Even though Germany's diesel car industry was dogged by scandal, with carmakers accused of cheating on emissions tests, 2017 was a breakout year. Porsche rival BMW wasn't far behind, announcing record bonuses of 9,455 Euros ($9,286) for each employee, while Daimler-owned Mercedes-Benz was dishing out 5,700 Euros ($5,598).

CHAPTER 39:

STORE LEFT OPEN BY MISTAKE, BUT ONLY CHERRY TOMATOES MISSING, AND THE CUSTOMER OVERPAYS

There's a holiday in Canada called Family Day, and we can only guess what it's all about. By the way, stores are normally closed across the land on that special day. But in Kingston, Ontario, one downtown grocery store had "customers" anyway when the doors to the business were mistakenly left open on the holiday.

Imagine if you showed up at your favorite store, and the doors were open, but there was nobody there to serve you. On February 18, 2019, the Food Basics shop located on Barrack Street was supposed to be shut down for the provincial holiday.

However, with practically all the area's grocery stores closed for the day, those searching for a few staples or dinner ingredients were indeed pleased to find the doors of the downtown grocer wide open - that is, until they got inside.

With no staff scheduled to work on the day, the welcoming open doors of the business allowed the general public to enter, but then, they weren't actually able to purchase any of their favorite items.

Nonetheless, numerous people enjoyed strolling around inside the store, some even unaware of the actual situation, while others gathered in front trying to figure out exactly what was going on.

"I was standing there trying to decide what to do, and a guy comes out of the store with two packages of cherry tomatoes," one eyewitness (who asked to stay unnamed) revealed. "So, I asked, 'Hey, buddy! You just taking some tomatoes?' He said, 'I left $5 on the counter.'"

The cherry-tomato witness decided to get in touch with Kingston Police to advise them of the store's status and the exiting tomatoes. According to Kingston Police, officers did arrive at the Food Basics store at about 4:25 p.m. on Family Day. Officers then contacted a surprised store manager, who quickly found that nothing out of the ordinary had happened.

"It looks as though there was no damage, and the situation wasn't out of control or anything," reported Constable Ashley Gutheinz, Kingston Police media relations officer. By the way, cherry tomatoes are normally picked by hand, and thus the labor cost adds a bit to the final price. Let's just say that the store probably broke even on this fresh tomato deal.

CHAPTER 40:

MINNESOTA PAYS HOMEOWNERS TO PLANT BEE-FRIENDLY FLOWERS

In January 2020, Minnesota announced a cool one million dollars in financial incentives urging people to turn their lawns into areas rich in wildflowers, clover, and native grasses - all bee-friendly plants. The state also began to ask residents to stop spraying so many nasty herbicides, hold off on cutting the grass so much, and let their lawns get back to more natural, wilder conditions.

The state's expressed objective was to "provide food sources for pollinators of all kinds, but would specifically aim at saving the rusty patched bumblebee, a fat and fuzzy species on the brink of extinction that seems to be making its final stand in the cities of the Upper Midwest," said a *Star Tribune* report.

Bumblebees are especially vital to the region, according to research, as they vibrate at a frequency that unleashes precious pollen -

other insects can't quite reach the desired frequency. The disappearance of native prairies and forests all across the country has made pollinators more reliant on urban and suburban lawn flowers, admitted James Wolfin, a bee habitat specialist at the University of Minnesota.

Wolfin's research has homed in on the presence of so-called "bee lawns," which are grassy stretches dotted and mixed with lots of small flowers like Dutch white clover, creeping thyme, self-heal, ground plum, and dandelions.

The flowers make excellent food sources for the busy bees, while at the same time being cheap to plant and easy to keep up. "A pound of Dutch white clover is about $7, and it grows low enough that people wouldn't even have to change the way they mow their lawns," Wolfin informed the *Star Tribune* and its curious readers.

Fully 55 of Minnesota's 350 bee species are dependent on white clover alone, he added. "So just by not treating white clover like a weed, and letting it grow in a yard provides a really powerful resource for nearly 20% of the bee species in the state," Wolfin concluded.

Did you have any idea that all those different types of bees were dive-bombing your backyard?

So, please let your yard go to the bees, and not only will you NOT need to spend so much time hunched over pulling weeds, but the insects will quickly thank you for your efforts (and you'll have more time to keep up with the news).

CHAPTER 41:

'TIGER KING' BILL PREVENTS PRIVATE OWNERSHIP OF BIG CATS

The House passed a bill in late 2020 that aims to prevent the rise of another "Tiger King." Joe Exotic - one more nickname for Tiger King Joseph Maldonado-Passage, after whom the notorious Netflix documentary series is named - now languishes in prison, serving a 22-year sentence for wildlife crimes, as well as a murder-for-hire scheme.

Some Congress folks wanted to be absolutely sure that nobody else will ever be allowed to permit the public to mess around with big cats like the Tiger King did at the former Greater Wynnewood Exotic Animal Park in Oklahoma.

Most of us have no desire to deal with anything bigger than our standard tabby cat. In this case, the House passed legislation known as the Big Cat Public Safety Act in an overwhelming 272-114 vote, which prohibits private ownership of big cats, such as "standard" tigers, lions, leopards, cheetahs, jaguars, and cougars.

The law makes it illegal for someone to raise or own big cats without an animal exhibition license from the U.S. Department of Agriculture. However, for all the granddads reading this, you'll be happy to know that the government will "grandfather" in current owners - if they register with the U.S. Fish and Wildlife Service and abide by federal regulations.

The bill's real impact on the Tiger King if he hadn't run into the financial and legal problems that forced him to transfer ownership of his zoo to Jeff Lowe, and eventually caused him to end up in the slammer - would have been nominal. Maldonado-Passage possessed an exhibitor's license, so he could've remained in operation, but would've needed to halt his polemical practice of "cub petting." The bill outlaws licensed exhibitors from allowing visitors to interact with such big cats.

Utah Republican Rob Bishop wasn't so quick to go along with the program. "This bill, contrary to what I've been hearing so far, is not about protecting the public from big cats," the opponent said. "It's about hurting small, family-run zoos across the country. It's a power play of some kind." Several Grand Old Party (GOP) lawmakers also made fun of the Democrats for bringing the bill to the floor before other actions such as coronavirus relief.

California Democrat Jared Huffman came down squarely on the side of the cats. "Through the drama and twists, it (*Tiger King*) showed a real issue: the inhumane exploitation of these majestic animals," Huffman claimed. "We're bringing the #BigCatPublicSafetyAct to end these practices up for a vote, and I'm glad to have helped move it forward through our committee."

In the meantime, Maldonado-Passage was busy posting on Instagram from jail, hoping that President Trump would pardon him, and promising that if he "escaped" his prison cell, his *Tiger King* days would definitively be done for good.

CHAPTER 42:

NASA "HUMAN COMPUTER" KATHERINE JOHNSON CELEBRATES HER 100TH BIRTHDAY

You may know somebody who is always struggling to remember where they put their keys. Then there's Katherine Johnson, allegedly a "human computer," who overcame racial and gender discrimination as a Black woman to become a critical cog in the USA's successful space program. In 2019, NASA participated in her 100th birthday celebrations.

Johnson became well known for her ability to calculate the complex orbital mechanics that allowed NASA to launch crewed missions into outer space for the very first time. She co-wrote no fewer than 26 scientific papers, as well as receiving the Presidential Medal of Freedom from President Obama in 2015.

Johnson developed a sterling reputation for her math skills (that went a bit beyond basic algebra) during her 35 years at NASA. Not only did Katherine's efforts help send the first American into space, but they also set the tone for the Space Shuttle Program, while nudging NASA into its transition to use real computers (not just human ones!).

Even though it's hard to believe nowadays, it was a fact that during the centenarian's early years at NASA, the space giant went along with state and federal segregation laws. That simply meant that Johnson and her African American workmates were all forced to use separate restrooms, while eating and working under "different" (and dare we say less comfortable) conditions, in contrast to their white colleagues.

What's more: can you believe that the office where Johnson performed some of her most brilliant calculations was called "Colored Computers"? During one specific assignment, her diligence and prowess in math took her to a new plane altogether. She assisted a male flight research team, and her reasoning skills made such an impression on her leaders that they simply "forgot" to send her back to the computing pool.

At the end of the day, NASA became desegregated, along with other federal agencies. But that didn't mean the gender and race barriers confronting Johnson and others just went away. At the time, women weren't allowed to sign their names to their reports, even if the work therein was done completely by them.

Not only was Johnson a brilliant mathematician but she also happened to be assertive and persistent. She ended up being the first female in her division to sign her name to a report when a male coworker declined to list his name on a study, which he admitted was done mostly by Johnson.

In the years that followed, Johnson helped NASA ring in the age of electronic computers. Her reputation for precision turned her into the best candidate to test the machines. Indeed, a guy named John Glenn (who you may have heard of) told NASA he wouldn't fly orbits around the Earth until the computer calculations were personally approved by Katherine.

Johnson's alma mater, West Virginia State University, revealed a statue of her likeness, and a STEM scholarship bearing her powerful name, on her 100th birthday. At the unveiling ceremony, former astronaut and keynote speaker Yvonne Cagle declared: "What makes Katherine so extraordinary is she not only prevailed while segregation failed. Dr. Johnson has continued to persevere and thrive with the gracious poise and clarity that defies mere words of explanation, let alone definition."

You can find out more about Johnson and her fellow mathematicians of color in the 2016 movie, *Hidden Figures*, based on Margot Lee Shetterly's book bearing the same name.

CHAPTER 43:

TWENTY-YEAR-OLD WINS $451-MILLION: WILL HELP FAMILY AND HUMANITY

Once upon a time, I won $35 in a weekly scratch lottery (after spending $5 every Friday for a year, which I later figured out was a total of $260.). So, we were all a bit surprised to catch a Florida Lottery news release early in 2018 telling us that 20-year-old Shane Missler, of Port Richey, claimed the jackpot from the multistate game's January 5 lucky draw.

Shane chose to receive his pot of gold in a one-time, lump-sum payment of $281,874,999 (if Missler had opted to receive the grand total in installments instead, he could've raked in some $451 million).

"I'm only 20, but I hope to use it to pursue a variety of passions, help my family, and do some good for humanity," Shane reported in a prepared statement. It might be a bit harder to talk to Mr. Missler in person these days after his great good fortune.

You're obviously curious to know the winning numbers, though they might not come up again in this sequence for a while. The magic combination of numbers that scored the nation's 10th-largest jackpot ever were 28-30-39-59-70, with a Mega Ball (whatever on earth that is) of 10.

The special ticket was issued at a no-frills 7-Eleven in Port Richey. The retailer was also set to receive a $100,000 bonus. *The Tampa Bay Times* claimed that Missler appeared grinning from ear to ear while securing a yellow envelope in which he turned in his ticket at the Florida Lottery HQ in Tallahassee. His dad and lawyer came along for the ride and released a statement on his behalf.

"If there's one thing, I have learned thus far in my short time on this earth it is that those who maintain a positive mindset and stay true to themselves get rewarded," Missler's statement read. "I look forward to the future." Believe us, Shane: your coffee's going to taste a lot sweeter tomorrow.

Lottery officials announced that the money would be paid into a trust, quickly established with Missler as the managing member, and cryptically named "Secret 007, LLC." "Although I'm young, I've had a crash course this week in financial management, and I feel so fortunate to have this incredible wealth and the team behind me," Missler declared. The youngster also informed the *Times* that he planned to move away from Port Richey.

"I intend to take care of my family, have some fun along the way, and cement a path for financial success so that I can leave a legacy far into the future." Port Richey and the local 7-Eleven will surely miss you and your regular business, Shane.

CHAPTER 44:

EIGHTY-TWO-YEAR-OLD YOUTUBER "SKYRIM GRANDMA" ADDED TO POPULAR ONLINE GAME

If you happened to see Shirley Curry pass by on the street, you probably wouldn't know that she's a YouTuber who's managed to attract almost a half million subscribers. She's 82 years old and boasts of having four sons and nine grandchildren (you'll find out by checking her YouTube bio, although she's unfortunately a widow as well).

In her spare time, Shirley loves to play and record video games. What's one of her all-time favorite games? *The Elder Scrolls 5: Skyrim*, of course.

Bethesda Softworks, the creator of the popular sci-fi role-play game (RPG), picked up on the great demand from fans to include Shirley as a possible NPC in future game development. And what in the world is an NPC, you dare to ask?

An NPC is a non-player character in such a game. NPCs are generally used to provide information or perform tasks for the player-character, and sometimes can be interacted with in the game itself.

Sure enough: during The Elder Scroll's 25th Anniversary stream in 2019, Bethesda announced that it would definitely make Curry into an NPC in the upcoming version, *The Elder Scrolls* 6. A video glancing back at the fandom generated by the series shows a clip of her character model being created.

"That petition for Skyrim Grandma we did hear, and she will be immortalized in the game," Bethesda's Todd Howard proclaimed during the live-streamed panel. "This means a lot to me because I would be extremely happy to know that somebody else was playing with my character in a future Elder Scrolls game," admitted Curry herself during a special video promoting the series.

The feeling is sweet: seeing footage of Bethesda actually inviting an elderly, sprightly Curry to its studio to capture her likeness for use in the game. You might also like to know how an 82-year-old grandma goes about becoming a renowned YouTuber.

She worked as a secretary, in a candy factory, and for several years as a women's clothing department associate at Kmart, before deciding to retire at age 55 in 1991. Curry got into gaming after her son schooled her about how to play the 1996 turn-based strategy video game known as *Civilization II*.

In 2011, she spent more and more time on YouTube following gaming channels, and in 2015, she uploaded her first *Skyrim* gameplay video. You know most of the rest.

CHAPTER 45:

UBER WORKERS ARE EMPLOYEES AND NEED HOLIDAY PAY, UK COURT DECIDES

Uber drivers need to be treated as regular workers, rather than as self-employed, the UK's Supreme Court ruled in 2016. The decision could mean that thousands of hustling Uber drivers are entitled to receive the minimum wage, holiday pay, and rest breaks too!

The ruling meant that the ride-hailing app faced a rather large compensation bill and had wider consequences for the so-called gig economy (and that's not just where you hang out to play music, but instead work different part-time jobs to make a living). Uber claimed the ruling focused on a limited number of drivers, and has now gone ahead and made changes to its business.

In this long-haul legal battle, Uber finally appealed to the Supreme Court, after biting the dust in three earlier rounds. Uber's share price dived in US trading since investors had to figure out what impact the UK ruling would have in general on the company's particular business model.

Two Uber drivers, James Farrar and Yaseen Aslam, spearheaded the move by challenging Uber in a 2016 employment tribunal, arguing they truly worked for Uber as employees. At the time, Uber stated that its drivers were self-employed, and thus the giant wasn't required to pay any minimum wage or holiday pay. C'mon Uber: don't be such a scrooge!

The two former drivers originally won in the employment tribunal against the ride-hailing app colossus in October 2016. They informed the BBC that they were both "thrilled and relieved" due to the ruling. "I think it's a massive achievement in a way that we were able to stand up against a giant," exclaimed Mr. Aslam, president of the App Drivers & Couriers Union (ADCU).

"We didn't give up, and we were consistent - no matter what we went through emotionally or physically or financially, we stood our ground," Aslam concluded.

CHAPTER 46:

DISNEY HEIR SAYS GIVE EXEC BONUSES TO LOWEST-PAID STAFF

Abigail Disney continued her criticism of exorbitant executive pay at her family's company in 2019. Shortly after she referred to the pay of Disney's top bananas as "insane," the granddaughter of the company's co-founder, Roy Disney, submitted an opinion piece to the *Washington Post*. She realized that she'd "struck a nerve with a Twitter thread about wage inequality at the Walt Disney Co."

"I believe that Disney could well lead the way, if its leaders so chose, to a more decent, humane way of doing business," she penned in her piece. She suggested that the company set aside half of the bonuses that its executives put in their pockets and then hand it out to the lowest-paid 10% of Disney's 200,000 employees.

Six of Disney's top executives, including CEO Bob Iger, got their hands on stock awards and options valued at a combined $62 million the previous year. That didn't include the extra bonuses - worth possibly millions of dollars more - earned by lower-level execs at the media and theme park behemoth.

"Besides, at the pay levels we're talking about, an executive giving up half his bonus has zero effect on his quality of life," Abigail wrote. "For the people at the bottom, it could mean a ticket out of poverty or debt. It could offer access to decent health care, or the education of a child."

Think about it, all you top dogs, if your quality of life doesn't change one iota, maybe it's high time to share the wealth with those less fortunate.

CHAPTER 47:

FREE TUITION FOR THOSE LESS PRIVILEGED IN WISCONSIN

The University of Wisconsin-Madison now offers free tuition and no fees for in-state students who come from households that make less than $56,000 a year, announced *The Associated Press* in early 2018.

Known as Bucky's Tuition Promise, the scheme was the most recent by a major university trying to make higher education more accessible and affordable for all students. Prior to the decision, in-state students at UW-Madison paid $10,533 a year in tuition and fees.

"Many low and middle-income families in Wisconsin simply don't know whether they can afford to come to UW-Madison," Chancellor Rebecca Blank remarked as she unveiled the program, according to the AP.

"Indeed, if they just read the popular press about student debt and sky-rocketing tuition, they will assume that they can't. We want to make it very clear to low and moderate-income families in Wisconsin that we're going to do everything we can to make this an affordable school," Blank continued.

Numerous programs making comparable promises are becoming increasingly popular throughout higher ed. Proponents claim that sky-high tuition costs are prohibiting students from going after degrees. Another six colleges in the Big Ten sports conference (to which UW-Madison also belongs) have offered similar deals.

At the same time, the university regent's finance committee also signed off on increasing non-resident and graduate tuition for three schools within the UW-Madison group. Now go get your degrees, you Wisconsin badgers and cheese heads (at least if you like the Green Bay Packers football team).

CHAPTER 48:

UKRAINIANS DON'T NEED VISAS TO MOVE TO IRELAND

In February of 2022, the very green country of Ireland announced it would waive visa requirements for Ukrainians trying to escape the embattled country in the wake of the Russian attack. The Taoiseach - in other words, the prime minister of that fair land - declared that refugees attempting to flee the country would be welcomed in Ireland.

During the initial Russian assault, Ukrainian President Volodymyr Zelensky asked his citizenry not to panic, declaring that they were "ready for anything." Widespread international repulsion of what the west termed an "unprovoked attack" by Russia quickly followed. Ryanair suspended all flights to and from Ukraine at that moment.

"People who are considering leaving Ukraine and travelling to Ireland may for the coming period do so without a visa if they judge it safe to travel. Those who travel to Ireland without a visa during this period will then have 90 days after arrival to regularize their position. This position will be kept under ongoing review with the impact monitored closely," the Irish release read.

The situation in Ukraine also encouraged other EU Member States to open their doors to help incoming refugees forced to take flight from the country in search of international refuge.

One poignant story was about Ukrainians Olga and her husband, who'd almost finished constructing a new house for themselves and their two children when suddenly the bombs began to rain down in early March 2022. Their village in the Odesa region happened to be near two military installations targeted by missiles. Since their new home had no basement, they had to take cover any way they could.

"We hid in the inner rooms of the house on the floor. I covered the children with mattresses and pillows. It was so stressful," recalled Olga, a 42-year-old teacher and accountant. "We couldn't stand it anymore, so we decided to leave."

Olga, her sister, their children, and in-laws - four adults and four kids in total - crammed into the small family car with as many warm clothes and the few belongings they could manage and headed for the border with Moldova. Thousands of others packed the roads, all trying to dodge the attacks at the same time. The 37-mile journey lasted more than 24 hours.

"When we first came here, we didn't know what to do, or where to rest, or where to eat. That was the toughest moment for us," Olga remembers. "We were unwashed, we hadn't eaten, and we had small kids with us who were crying the whole trip."

More than 460,000 refugees from Ukraine; mostly women, children, and older people – have made it into Moldova since the start of the conflict. While many continued on to Romania and other EU countries, Olga and her children stayed together with almost 100,000 who chose to remain in Ukraine's smallest neighbor.

Despite the difficulties for a small country, with a population of around 2.7 million and restricted resources, Moldova and its citizens have opened their doors to the hard-pressed refugees.

Ukrainians enjoy the right to live and work in the country, as well as access vital services such as health care and education. Nearly 95% of the arrivals are being hosted by generous Moldovan families.

CHAPTER 49:

NO MORE CONFEDERATE NAMES FOR ARMY BASES SAYS SENATE

Southern General Robert E. Lee's time is up. The Senate overwhelmingly approved a defense bill in 2020 that included Senator Elizabeth Warren's (D-MA) provision requiring the U.S. military to rename its bases previously named after Confederate army generals.

The bill passed by a resounding vote of 86-14. That's neatly called "a veto-proof majority" that overrode President Trump's attempt to stave off the measure, which he'd previously talked loudly about doing at the end of June when Warren came forth with her proposal.

The Black Lives Matter protests across the nation, triggered by the police killing of George Floyd, provided a fresh force after years of frustrated efforts to move ahead with the base-name changes. The majority believe it was improper for the U.S. military to highlight individuals who battled to the death in support of slavery, as well as seeking to secede from the U.S.

Although in the past the military resisted those calls, more recently Secretary of Defense Mark Esper and Secretary of the Army Ryan D. McCarthy became reportedly "open to the idea."

The esteemed Chairman of the Senate Armed Services Committee, Senator Jim Inhofe, a Republican from "The Sooner State" of Oklahoma, declared that both House and Senate lawmakers would work to produce a bill "that both sides can support, and the president can sign."

Now that's the way a bipartisan government is supposed to work for the benefit of everyone in the nation.

CHAPTER 50:

FOUR-DAY WORKWEEK MEANS MORE PRODUCTIVE, LESS STRESSED EMPLOYEES

So, you say you want to work four days a week but get paid for five? It appears almost too good to be true. Yet companies around the world that have already cut something off their working week also have discovered that it leads to higher productivity, more motivated staff, and less burnout.

"It is much healthier, and we do a better job if we're not working crazy hours," claimed Jan Schulz-Hofen, founder of the Berlin-based project management software company Planio. The firm presented a four-day work week to the company's 10 staff members in 2018.

In New Zealand, trust company Perpetual Guardian announced a decrease in stress, together with a boost in staff engagement, after it decided on a 32-hour week earlier in the same year. Even in work-obsessed Japan, the government is encouraging companies to permit Monday mornings off, although other schemes in that country to persuade employees to take it easy haven't had too much effect.

Britain's Trades Union Congress (TUC) is agitating for the whole country to move to a four-day week by the end of this century, an initiative supported by the (ironically named) opposition Labour Party.

The TUC says simply that a shorter week is one way for workers to share in the wealth that's generated by new technologies, such as machine learning and robotics. It's seen as similar to the way they won the right to have the weekend off after the industrial revolution took hold in the 1930s.

Lucie Greene, a trends expert at the J. Walter Thompson consulting company, spoke of a growing backlash against overwork, underlined by waves of criticism after Tesla boss Elon Musk tweeted that "nobody ever changed the world on 40 hours a week." (We're also wondering if anybody ever changed the world while spending most of their waking hours on Twitter.)

"People are starting to take a step back from the 24-hour digital life we have now, and realize the mental health issues from being constantly connected to work," Greene pointed out.

A recent survey of 3,000 employees in eight countries, including the U.S., Britain, and Germany, found that nearly half thought they could comfortably finish their tasks in a mere five hours a day if they didn't have to deal with interruptions.

But many are going beyond 40 hours a week anyway, with the U.S. leading the way, where 49% claimed they worked overtime. Some habits are hard to break.

CHAPTER 51:

CHILE OPTS FOR 11 MILLION ACRES OF NEW NATIONAL PARKS

Chile decided to set aside 11 million acres of land for national parks, helped by the biggest-ever land donation from a private entity to a country, in early 2017. The special conservation efforts of the Tompkins Foundation helped lay the groundwork for Chile to greatly improve and increase its protection of the pristine Patagonia wilderness.

Established by Kristine McDivitt Tompkins, the previous CEO of Patagonia, and the late Doug Tompkins, the co-founder of North Face and Esprit, the Tompkins Foundation allowed the couple, well known for purchasing large chunks of land in Patagonia, to realize their ambition of conserving the vast Patagonian wilderness for generations to come.

On the other hand, their efforts weren't always considered the best by the Chilean government and its citizens. The Tompkins couple was even accused of trying to split Chile into two and form a new state. They were even viewed as CIA spies intending to infiltrate the Chilean government.

After decades, they gradually gained the trust of Chile, and their intentions were finally seen as well-founded. The move to donate one million acres of land to the Chilean government ultimately solidified their relations with the country of Chile.

Sadly, Doug Tompkins wasn't able to fully enjoy the culmination of his decades of work. In 2015, he passed away as a result of severe hypothermia after a kayaking accident.

"I know that if Doug were here today, he would speak of national parks being one of the greatest expressions of democracy that a country can realize, preserving the masterpieces of a nation for all of its citizenry," Kristine McDivitt Tompkins stated, recalling her late husband.

The expanded parks will surely aid Chile's ecotourism efforts, generating an estimated $270 million per year in revenue while providing more than 40,000 jobs to locals. The newly protected areas cover a diverse collection of ecosystems in Chile's long, spectacular landmass, from deserts to volcanoes to rainforests.

With this impressive addition of national park acreage, Chile scales the ranks of nations that possess the highest percentage of protected land, comparable to Costa Rica, "the rich coast."

CHAPTER 52:

ARMY AWARDS THREE HERO MEDALS TO TEENS POSTHUMOUSLY

Peter Wang was a 15-year-old member of the Junior ROTC. He was killed trying to help his fellow students escape a mass shooting in Parkland, Florida. Peter was posthumously admitted to the U.S. Military Academy in 2018.

Along with two other freshman cadets, Martin Duque and Alaina Petty, both 14, Peter was also awarded the Medal of Heroism - the top medal granted to Junior Army Reserve Officers' Training Corps cadets.

"It was an appropriate way for USMA to honor this brave young man," said the academy in a statement. "West Point has given posthumous offers of admissions in very rare instances for those candidates or potential candidates whose actions exemplified the tenets of duty, honor, and country."

Peter was wearing his gray Junior ROTC shirt when he was shot down while he held the door open allowing others to escape a gunman who killed 17 people at Marjory Stoneman Douglas High School. His classmates and family members recalled that Peter's burning desire was to attend West Point. His ultimate admission to the academy came on the same day as his funeral.

"He saved people's lives," stated Victoria Downing at Peter's funeral service, in the words of the Sun Sentinel. She was one of Peter's awed and saddened classmates. "He deserves it."

"Wang was buried Tuesday in uniform, at his family's request, and the JROTC Heroism Medal was on his uniform," Lt. Col. Christopher Belcher, spokesman for Army Cadet Command, declared. A second medal was given to the family as a keepsake. A medal was also awarded to Petty's family at Alaina's service.

CHAPTER 53:

NO MORE PLASTIC BAGS
AT KROGER CHECKOUT

Kroger informed the world that it'll ban all plastic checkout bags by the year 2025. This is America's largest supermarket chain talking: it will change from single-use to reusable bags, and in the process eliminate 123 million pounds of garbage annually sent to bulging landfills. That number will quadruple the volume of plastic the retailer currently recycles.

As we speak, Kroger sells reusable bags beginning at a single buck apiece. Kroger also plans to ramp up the availability of those bags. For the foreseeable future, shoppers will still have the choice of requesting paper bags.

The supermarket giant said it's also looking into cutting back on or phasing out plastic bags used to wrap produce and meat, but it's really focusing on eliminating checkout bags for the time being. The ban will directly affect a wide range of consumers: Kroger serves nine million customers every day at its 2,800 stores in 35 states, including the District of Columbia.

Kroger's Seattle-based QFC subsidiary, with 63 stores serving the Pacific Northwest, was the first group to eliminate the bags by 2019. In addition to the hundreds of its namesake stores across the Midwest and South, Kroger operates many more under the titles of Harris Teeter, Ralphs (we always wondered about what happened to the apostrophe here), Fred Meyer, and Fry's, as well as other "nameplates."

Kroger officials made it clear that they're responding to the ever-growing environmental concerns brought up by shoppers, employees, communities, and non-profits. Hey, that's us!

CHAPTER 54:

LEBRON JAMES WORKS TO BOOST THE BLACK VOTE

Besides throwing down monster dunks, blocking high-flying opponents' shots, and scowling at anybody and anything that gets in his way, NBA star LeBron James has also turned his efforts toward helping more Black people vote, and thus change their lives for the better.

LeBron James declared that he and several other pro athletes planned to kick-start a charitable organization that would protect Black American voting rights, five months before the presidential election back in 2020, according to *The New York Times* (not the N.Y. Knicks, mind you).

The move came as massive protests swept the U.S. and the world, demanding a halt to hundreds of years of racial discrimination against Black people and people of color. "We feel like we're getting some ears and some attention, and this is the time for us to finally make a difference," James informed the *Times*.

The organization, called 'More Than A Vote', aims to coax more African Americans to register to vote, and especially to show up at the polls for the November 3 (2020) elections. The group also vowed to battle against other factors that contribute to African American disenfranchisement (like previous arrests that prevent Black people from voting in some states).

"Yes, we want you to go out and vote, but we're also going to give you the tutorial," James said to the *Times*. "We're going to give you the background on how to vote, and what they're trying to do, the other side, to stop you from voting."

With upward of 135 million followers on Twitter, Instagram, and Facebook, James wants to take advantage of social media to condemn attempts to restrict voting by racial minorities. King James himself agreed to finance the project, together with hoop players Trae Young and Jalen Rose, football player Alvin Kamara, and comedian Kevin Hart.

The organization plans to work with other get-out-the-vote groups, including When We All Vote and Fair Fight. This particular voting movement isn't the L.A. Laker's first political adventure. In 2016, James took part in a campaign event for the presidential candidate, Democrat Hillary Rodham Clinton.

This isn't LeBron's first charitable challenge either: he's made university scholarships available via the LeBron James Family Foundation, and also established a school for third to eighth graders in his home state of Ohio, the beloved "Land of the Buckeyes."

CHAPTER 55:

HOW TO STOP HATE WITH KINDNESS

One Black man has single-handedly made more than 200 white racists leave the Ku Klux Klan by simply confronting their prejudice and racism with his friendship and kindness.

This is the short story of Daryl Davis, 58, blues musician and inspirational author, who journeyed all around the U.S. since the early 1980s actively searching for and making friends with members of the clearly racist organization. Just to remind you: founded in 1865, the KKK is a white supremacy cult that organizes its members to persecute people for their skin color and religious beliefs.

Nonetheless, Daryl Davis continues to face the hatred and respond to a call he first felt as a young man when he made up his mind to confront the KKK's ideology head-on, one single member at a time. He's documented his amazing mission in a book called *Klan-*

destine Relationships: A Black Man's Odyssey in the Ku Klux Klan. An updated version was re-released in 2017.

Originally from the "Windy City" of Chicago, Daryl also made the time to carve out a noteworthy music career playing the blues and R&B, while stepping onstage with the likes of Jerry Lee Lewis, Chuck Berry, and even ex-President Bill Clinton. The legendary Muddy Waters was one of Davis's friends.

Daryl claims: "Music absolutely played a massive role in bridging many gaps in the racial divides I would encounter. Once when I was performing in a predominantly white venue, a white man approached me on my break, put his arm around me and exclaimed, 'This is the first time I've ever heard a black man play the piano like Jerry Lee Lewis.'"

CHAPTER 56:

KELLOGG'S TURNS REJECTED CORNFLAKES INTO BEER

Consumers (like you and me) who're worried about the damage caused by their carbon footprint can now drink beer and ease their guilt over the environment at the same time. Kellogg's has released a beer made from leftover cornflakes.

Cereal monster Kellogg's and Salford-based brewery Seven Bro7hers in the UK got together to craft a beer using cornflakes that were considered either too big, too small, or overcooked to get through quality control.

The beer's called 'Throw Away IPA', and is designed to help the cereal maker drastically reduce its food waste. Seven Bro7hers, a craft brewery located in Salford, Manchester, decided to swap out about 30% of their usual mash recipe for cornflakes.

The brew guys started with around 132 pounds of rejected cornflakes for the beer and announced that 10 pence (10 cents) from each can sold would be handed over to the food distribution charity FareShare.

Kellogg's first talked with Seven Bro7hers earlier in 2018 when the brewer collaborated with BrewDog Manchester to create a cornflake milkshake IPA. That sounds like a must-have beverage to add to your shopping list. On top of it all, Kellogg's already reduced its food waste by 12.5% during the year.

Kate Prince (no relation to the Minnesota musician), corporate social responsibility manager for Kellogg's in the UK, announced: "Kellogg's is always exploring different and sustainable ways to reduce food waste in its factories. So, it's great to be involved in such a fun initiative with a local supplier.

"Kellogg's is working hard to eliminate food waste in our manufacturing processes and give our consumers the wholesome products they love, with minimum impact on the planet. Our approach has delivered a 12.5 per cent reduction in food waste in our UK sites this year," she proudly concluded.

CHAPTER 57:

A MAN HELPS GRANDMA FIGHT DEMENTIA WITH JELLY DROPS

It may not seem so at first glance, but people with dementia often forget to drink water. As result, many dementia victims get dehydrated. But that part of the condition is often overlooked since the symptoms of dehydration are often confused with those of their mental condition.

When Lewis Hornby perceived that his grandmother wasn't drinking enough water, he searched for a solution. What he ended up inventing were "treats" that he refers to as Jelly Drops - brightly colored "candy-like" liquid balls that are a cinch to swallow and hydrate at the same time.

"For people with dementia, the symptoms of dehydration are often mistakenly attributed to their underlying condition, meaning it can easily go unnoticed until it becomes life-threatening," Hornby wrote.

"About a year ago, my grandma was unexpectedly rushed to hospital. She was found to be severely dehydrated. Thankfully, after 24 hours of IV fluids, she was back to her normal happy self, and is still enjoying a good quality of life to this day."

How did he make the Jelly Drops so effective, you`re tempted to ask? Horby checked with psychologists and hung out at a dementia care home to fully develop the product. The treats are composed of gelling agents, electrolytes, and 90% water. They look just like candies, an aspect that's also engaging for dementia patients.

The moment Hornby first presented them to his grandmother, she duly snatched them up. "When first offered, Grandma ate seven Jelly Drops in 10 minutes, the equivalent to a cup full of water, something that would usually take hours, and require much more assistance," Hornby recalled.

CHAPTER 58:

TURKISH MOM READS TO BLIND DAUGHTER AND THEN GETS HONORARY DEGREE

Most of us are glad to admit that our moms (or maybe our dads) helped us with at least one homework assignment (or three) over the years. But not many of us can claim that one of our parents read every book and helped with each homework assignment on our behalf for four full years of rigorous university.

Of course, you know that university can be a lot of fun, and many students relax after getting into a "tough school." In this phase, when youth is fully experienced and the taste of freedom is ever-present, lessons are sometimes a secondary concern.

Berru Merve Kul, 22, living in Kocaeli, Turkey, was accepted at Sakarya University in 2018, but she had a difficult road ahead of her as she's visually impaired. Fortunately, her mother was with her every step of the way for four years and even graduated together with her daughter, in a manner of speaking.

During her four-year university journey, Berru's mom Havva provided her eyes, feet, and hands, while constantly accompanying her dedicated daughter. The mother helped her daughter do her daily homework and successfully pass the exams by reading all her books and notes, the entire time.

Four years later, Berru Merve Kul graduated from the school. Merve was certainly not alone in the Sakarya University Faculty of Law Building on graduation day: she was with her mother again. Havva Kul took the stage along with her daughter to throw a cap, experiencing the excitement of graduation. They both got to throw caps.

Merve Kul received the graduation certificate she deserved at the end of four years, while her mother Havva was given an honorary graduation certificate for her four years of constant commitment. Feel free to check out the tweet shared by many on social media: daughter and mother flinging graduation caps together with glee.

CHAPTER 59:

COLORADO GRANDDAD COMES OUT OF THE CLOSET AT AGE 90

While most of us stayed in during the coronavirus pandemic, Kenneth Felts decided to come out. After hiding his sexuality for 90 years, the Arvada father and grandfather took advantage of his Covid-19 isolation to pen his memoirs. For the first time, in its pages, he admitted that he's gay.

After he delivered the news to his daughter, he shared it with everyone in a Facebook message that went viral. The story was reported by news agencies around the world, and Felts has since spoken on the BBC, Australian TV, and several U.S. shows.

"Having come out when I did, has been the highlight of the rest of my life, I guess. I've never enjoyed so much love from unknown people all over the world," *FOX31* heard from Felts. Messages of support on social media from well-wishers around the globe kept rolling in.

A Korean War veteran who was married years ago, Felts confessed how perplexed he was at first due to all the interest in his story. "I'm just an old guy who's 90 who decided to get off the closet floor and walk out the door," Felts said with a chuckle.

LGBTQ History Month happens in October and includes "National Coming Out Day." U.S. census data claims there are around three million LGBTQ adults over the age of 50 now residing in the U.S., and the figure should increase to about 7 million by 2030.

However, elderly members of the LGBTQ community are twice as likely to be single and live alone, four times less likely to have kids, and way more likely than heterosexuals to have confronted discrimination, prejudice, and stigma in social circles.

Even so, leaving the closet at the tender age of 90 is not quite as unusual as you may think. "Some folks might come out after their spouse has passed away. I believe coming out is a process," Reynaldo Mireles, director of elder services at The Center on Colfax, stated.

"I know that there are people who want to have relationships, and may feel like they're too old, but I believe you can find love at any moment in your life," Mireles added. We love that thought.

CHAPTER 60:

YOUTH PREFER WATCHING EARTH PROGRAMS TO *X FACTOR*

Apparently, the UK's younger citizens are finally in favor of the natural world's beauty rather than the shrieking of amateur singers. In December 2016, the BBC confirmed that the initial three episodes of *Planet Earth II* drew more viewers in the 16-to-34 age bracket than ITV's *The X Factor*.

Sir David Attenborough gave due credit to technology improvements, as the show experienced increased appeal in its second season, by bringing animals much closer to viewers than ever before. This was made possible by the use of remote cameras, which turned the creatures' habitats into stunning high-definition homes.

"I'm told that we're attracting a larger than the normal number of younger viewers, and apparently the music of Hans Zimmer in particular is striking a chord. That pleases me enormously," said the naturalist to the *Radio Times*.

Beyond the tech and sound editing improvements, Attenborough believes viewers are basically "reconnecting with a planet whose beauty is blemished, and whose health is failing," while coming to grips with the idea that their futures and that of the planet are inevitably linked.

The best ratings for *Planet Earth I"* to date came for the mountain-centric second episode, bringing in 1.8 million young viewers, compared to 1.4 million for The X Factor the same week. *The Times* and ITV had similar figures, although the former claimed a smaller margin.

"Visually, where Planet Earth took an almost God-like perspective and said, 'Let's look down on the Earth, and see the scale of the planet', what Planet Earth II is doing is saying, 'Let's get ourselves into the lives of the animals, and see it from their perspective,'" remarked Mike Gunton, series producer.

"The visual signature of the series is that you feel like the camera is with the animals. It's very fluid, very active. For example, you might see this wonderful lemur leaping through the forest. Normally when we'd film that, we'd be standing back observing it. But here the lemur almost jumps over your shoulder, and as it's jumping over your shoulder, you're with it - the camera is running with it!" Gunton gushed.

We could've sworn a lemur just sprinted through our studio as we wrote this.

CHAPTER 61:

IRISH TEEN WINS SCIENCE CONTEST REVEALING FAKE VIDEOS

Nowadays, when we listen to and watch the news, can we really be sure what we're hearing and seeing isn't fake? Well, maybe now there's hope for all of us, as a teenage Irish student won a national science contest for developing a method that can more easily expose "deepfake" online videos.

From County Cork in Ireland, Greg Tarr was named the winner of the 2021 BT Young Scientist & Technologist of the Year award for his pet project, Towards Deepfake Detection.

"Deepfake" videos and audio files can be changed using Artificial Intelligence (AI) to make it appear as if someone said or did something that they actually haven't.

The rapid spread of deepfake videos, which happens when such clips "go viral" and are quickly sent by viewers to others without checking their authenticity, has created international headaches in an era of digital news consumption, and social media players have been subject to fresh scrutiny. How can they better deal with this growth of misinformation?

One particular altered video, which purported to show U.S. President-elect Joe Biden drifting off during a TV interview, was widely spread prior to the election in November 2020. Talking to *Euronews*, Tarr claimed he'd developed an advanced AI application to help detect when videos have been modified.

"I've been working on AI for maybe four years, and it's being trained to look at vast amounts of data," remarked Tarr. "It's a concept that's currently being done, but mine is ten times faster. It's amazing how few people understand how prevalent deepfakes are in current media," he confirmed.

The 17-year-old student was anxious to demonstrate his work at the European Union's Contest for Young Scientists. "I look forward to representing my country in September with the same project, or maybe an improved version, and I'm also looking forward to commercializing or 'productizing' this development," Tarr stated.

CHAPTER 62:

GET THAT STYROFOAM OUT OF THE BIG APPLE!

New York City announced its official enforcement of a ban on styrofoam in early 2019. From now on, if anybody in the Big Apple tries to give you your take-out order in a styrofoam container, you'd better take cover!

The city outlawed the offending material on January 1, 2019. However, businesses were still given a six-month transition period before the real crackdown began. The ban mostly impacted food enterprises that used styrofoam for take-outs or big beverages.

It also prohibits stores from selling "packing peanuts"—you know, those fluffy white plastic pellets that go all over the place when you receive a package. Businesses were encouraged to change to materials that can be "composted," including paper.

"The City That Never Sleeps" decided to ban styrofoam, also known as polystyrene, because the material cannot be "recycled in a manner that is economically feasible" or "environmentally effective" in the metro area's recycling program. Bad guys would be fined $250 for the first offense, $500 for a second offense, and a hefty $1,000 for third offenses and more.

"New York City's ban on styrofoam is long overdue, and New Yorkers are ready to start using recyclable alternatives," New York Mayor Bill de Blasio declared in 2018 while announcing the details of the ban. "There's no reason to continue allowing this environmentally unfriendly substance to flood our streets, landfills, and waterways."

New York's styrofoam ban made it the largest U.S. city to outlaw the no-good material. Other cities that have joined the ban include San Diego, Miami, Seattle, and Washington, DC. The material is environmentally unfriendly since it rapidly separates into smaller pieces and is thus tough to clean up. It also sucks up toxins faster than other plastics. What's more: it's simply not biodegradable.

The grand state of Maine simultaneously announced it would outlaw styrofoam food containers starting in 2021. Maryland also prohibited the material's use. But at the end of the day, the "Free State" is pretty lenient and gave businesses a full year to comply. The Nutmeggers in Connecticut were also considering a ban.

CHAPTER 63:

NEW ZEALAND BUYS VACCINES FOR NEIGHBORS, INCLUDING SAMOA AND TONGA

Was it State Farm Insurance that used to sing about being "like a good neighbor"? New Zealand showed its neighborly approach in late 2020 and purchased enough Covid-19 vaccines to cover its Pacific Island brethren, including the nations of Samoa and Tonga.

The New Zealand government declared it had signed two more pre-purchase agreements for Covid-19 vaccines, allowing the country to start vaccinating its whole population in mid-2021.

Foreign Minister Nanaia Mahuta also emphasized that New Zealand would buy sufficient vaccines for the so-called New Zealand Realm countries - Tokelau, Niue, and the Cook Islands, to be precise - as well as neighbors Tonga, Samoa, and Tuvalu, if those countries were ready and willing to take up the offer.

The Kiwi government earmarked $75 million in development assistance money to support those countries in rolling out the life-saving vaccine. "Pacific countries have worked hard to keep Covid-19 out, or to stamp it out, and New Zealand has been committed to supporting them in this," mentioned Mahuta in his official statement.

"But their success has been hard-won. A safe and effective vaccine will be key to the region's economic and social recovery." About $10 million of the $75 million in assistance funding was destined for the global COVAX facility, which was striving to grant equal-access vaccines to nations around the world.

Covid-stricken countries were urgently vaccinating their populations, as the virus spread and mortality mounted. The UK at the time had vaccinated 130,000 people, initially with the Pfizer-BioNTech vaccine. The country went into lockdown over the winter to fend off the virus's spread.

While Covid-19 deaths in the U.S. climbed, the Food and Drug Administration there gave the green light for the first health workers to get the jab. Amazingly, New Zealand had no cases of Covid-19 at that moment in late 2020, and only 43 cases existed within quarantine facilities at the country's borders.

CHAPTER 64:

NINE-YEAR-OLD COLLECTS CANS AND DONATES PROCEEDS, ALL ON HIS OWN

There's a special place in Illinois called Carterville where a nine-year-old kid is doing his best to help his community, and at the same time help the environment where he lives. Draegan Bandy spends his spare time "canning" and not necessarily for his own gain.

"We collect cans. We don't really choose the type of cans we collect, but it has to be made of tin. So, we find the cans, we put them in a garbage bag, and once we get a few bags, or enough that it's worth something," Bandy explained.

Normally, Bandy takes a few months to collect enough cans before carting them to the recycling center. They're worth 40 cents a pound. "I've always had a thing to collect shiny things, so I collect cans and stuff. Once in a while, I'll find pieces of metal, parts of cans - you take those, too. I decided to start doing cans because that was a pretty big money-maker," enthused Draegan.

But he's not really hoarding that money just for himself. Bandy recalled, "I donated $60 to Honor Flight. I have a hatpin right here from it. That was my reward for doing that. The other reward that I actually cherish more than the hat pin is the fact that I can help someone else."

Kristina Austin, the Event Coordinator for Veteran's Honor Flight in Southern Illinois, affirmed that each and every donation makes a difference. "We were very honored for this nine-year-old boy to make that decision to choose to donate to us. He said his grandfather was a veteran, and so he was just really excited to be involved."

"I mean, I'm not okay with people throwing out cans, but it's a good business for me because it's helping out other people. It's helping out them, it's helping out the Earth because I don't want the Earth to die," pointed out Draegan. The Bandy boy has also given money to Toys for Tots and the Cambria

Toy Drive, and his next donation will apparently work toward helping the homeless.

CHAPTER 65:

FOUR TEENS RESCUE 90-YEAR-OLD NEIGHBOR FROM BURNING HOME

Oklahoma resident Catherine Ritchie lived cozily in the same home in the Tulsa suburb of Sapulpa for 58 years. That all changed in May 2019. While in the bathroom getting ready for bed, she turned around and witnessed the head of her bed on fire, according to TV station KTUL. That's when her heroes came to the rescue.

All between the ages of 14 and 17, four boys living nearby happened to be outside on their way to a convenience store when they noticed the horrendous smell. "It smelled kind of like burning rubber," Dylan Wick, 16, informed the Tulsa station. "Then we heard the house alarm go off."

Catherine stayed inside to battle the fire. But she quickly decided against it, phoned 911, and pressed her emergency call button. Suddenly another problem cropped up. "The smoke was so bad, I couldn't see to get out of my room," she remembered. "I felt along the wall, and I went into the closet instead of the door to get out of the room. I finally did get to the door."

At the same time, she tried to feel her way out of the house, the boys leapt into action, and attempted to bust down the doors to get inside. One of the lads, 14-year-old Nick Byrd, made it through the back door and ran inside. He found Catherine dazed in the hallway, lost in the smoke.

"This young boy was right there. He picked me up, and I said, 'I can walk,' and he said, 'we're getting out of here,'" Catherine recalled.

"I just kind of heard her. I went to the right of the house and no one was there," said Byrd. "I went to the left of the house, and I saw her in the hallway, so I just grabbed her and took her to Seth."

Catherine and her heroes all got out safely, and firefighters managed to halt the flames before they maliciously spread. The boys returned to the partially burned home soon after to see the damage and reflect on what happened only weeks earlier.

"Ever since that night, my life has just changed...for the better," declared 17-year-old Wyatt Hall while glancing at a burned mattress. Catherine admits she's forever grateful. "That's what I have to think. They were just special, as young as they were," the senior citizen enthused.

One of Catherine's daughters crafted a blog post thanking the four boys for rescuing the damsel in distress, her mom.

CHAPTER 66:

HUMPBACK WHALES ON THE COMEBACK TRAIL

We're happy to report that humpback whales were removed from Australia's threatened-species list in February 2022. The government's independent science panel dealing with threatened species assessed that the mammals had made a significant comeback.

Whaling activities had driven the species to near extinction. However, since the 1980s, when the practice was mostly phased out, the whale population grew considerably. On the other hand, conservationists warn that even though their numbers have bounced back, these massive mammals still confront major risks, among them pollution and climate change.

Environment Minister Susan Ley said the change followed advice that she had received from the independent Threatened Species

Scientific Committee that the humpback whale population was now strong enough for them to be removed from the list.

"They looked at issues of climate change, and they looked at issues of krill fisheries, as well as all of the other circumstances of the population trends for the species," she explained. "Most of the listings I make are up-listings or introducing species and ecological communities onto the list for the first time. So, it's really encouraging to see a strong conservation story that leads to a species actually coming off that list."

Ms. Ley remarked that while the species had been "delisted" it was still given protection in Australian waters under the Environment Protection and Biodiversity Conservation (EPBC) Act, due to its listing as a migratory species and a cetacean.

That status makes it a criminal offense to kill, injure, take, trade, keep, move, or interfere with a humpback. In other words, don't mess with these whales (besides snapping a picture or two).

Marine scientist Vanessa Pirotta from Macquarie University said the delisting could help drive more focus - and funding - to whale species that hadn't bounced back as strongly post-whaling.

"There's been this momentum to celebrate the conservation of these animals, but then also reassess their listing in terms of the protection," Dr. Pirotta elaborated. "Ongoing cautious monitoring will remain for these populations, allowing us to focus our conservation dollars into protecting other species such as the Southern Right Whale."

But Dr. Pirotta warned the delisting didn't mean that authorities could take it easy, with whales facing many threats, especially from climate change. "Some of the threats that whales face globally include ship strike, entanglement in fishing gear, acoustic pollution, marine pollution, and of course, climate change," the good doctor said.

"Climate change is a really big one because this influences where these animals might go, where prey distributions are, and unfortunately, a reduction in sea ice means a reduction in Antarctic krill habitat which is one of the primary food sources of these humpback whale populations.

"It's a bittersweet situation because you've got a recovering whale population, which is a great thing, but also we should be cautiously optimistic as well as to adhere to monitoring this population in the future," Dr. Pirotta concluded.

This uplifting story is "to be continued," as we say.

CHAPTER 67:

AFGHAN TRANSLATOR SAVES US LIVES, AND THEN BECOMES AN AMERICAN CITIZEN

Janis Shinwari celebrated his first Independence Day as an American citizen at age 42. His journey to the U.S. started on the battlefield in his native Afghanistan. Shinwari served for nine years as a translator for U.S. military forces, realizing all the while that he was risking his life, and endangering his family.

During that span, Shinwari saved the lives of several U.S. soldiers, including one who helped bring Shinwari and his family to the U.S. "If I was in Afghanistan - if I didn't come here, I wouldn't be alive now. I would be dead," Shinwari admitted to *CNN Heroes* in 2018.

At the time, he recalled his decision to side with U.S. soldiers after seeing the Taliban regime's terror in person. Shinwari knew the U.S. needed translators, but he also understood the risks.

"If the Taliban catch you, they will torture you in front of your kids and families, and make a film of you, and then send it to other translators as a warning message to stop working with the American forces," explained Shinwari.

Acting Homeland Security Deputy Secretary Ken Cuccinelli administered the oath of allegiance to Shinwari and his wife in Fairfax, Virginia. Cuccinelli honored Shinwari for his service and for saving the lives of five American soldiers.

During one terrible battle in April 2008, Shinwari helped save the life of Captain Matt Zeller, an American soldier he had only met a few days earlier. Zeller's unit was on routine patrol near the village of Waghez in Ghazni province when the Taliban attacked. They lost a vehicle, and quickly found themselves outnumbered and outgunned.

In 2018, Zeller told *CNN Heroes* that he was knocked out when a mortar round exploded, throwing him into a ditch. As he regained his senses, he believed he was about to die.

"I was going to make sort of peace with my fate, and I was going to go out fighting," he recalled.

What Zeller didn't perceive was that two Taliban fighters were approaching him. That's when Shinwari, who had been crawling through nearby bushes, shot and killed them. Zeller remembered Shinwari standing above him and saying, "I'm Janis. And I'm one of your translators. You're not safe." Shinwari recalled getting Zeller to safety, thus creating a powerful bond.

"Since that time, we become even closer than brothers," Shinwari stressed. After that, the Taliban placed Shinwari on a hit list that singled out translators working with U.S. troops. He reached out to Zeller to help him secure a visa to come to the U.S. Shinwari said he expected the ordeal to "take a couple of months. But it took years."

All that while, the 38-year-old Zeller worked tirelessly to help Shinwari. He launched a Change.org petition and contacted all his connections in Congress. "I just basically asked anyone who would listen, 'Will you help me?' I owe this person my life. I'm willing to do whatever it takes. I will cash in and call in whatever favor. I will owe whatever it is that I need to owe. Tell me what it is that I need to do to get you to help me,'" Zeller related to CNN.

In 2013, Shinwari and his family finally obtained visas. Once in the United States, Zeller helped the Shinwaris settle into their new home. He assisted Shinwari in finding a job, getting a car, and guiding the Shinwaris through their first year in the U.S. Zeller even established a GoFundMe campaign that raised $35,000 for the Shinwaris' expenses.

But Shinwari often thought of the other translators who were still at risk in Afghanistan and Iraq. "We are happy. But I'm not happy about my coworkers, about my brothers and sisters that served the U.S. government in Afghanistan and Iraq, and they are still left behind," he exclaimed. "I will fight for them, to get them here. And we will not stop fighting. It doesn't matter how long it takes. But I will fight for them."

Shinwari and Zeller decided to use part of the money to create No One Left Behind, a non-profit organization that's helped thousands of combat translators relocate to the U.S.

The group has aided more than 5,000 translators and their families come to the U.S., leading them through the visa process. The organization provides resettlement and support services upon their arrival, such as locating permanent housing, home furnishings, job placement, and improving language skills.

"I will not stop fighting until I get the last translator who's left behind," Shinwari stressed. "I promise them that I will never forget about my brothers and sisters that are still left behind in Iraq and Afghanistan."

CHAPTER 68:

SOBER 30 YEARS, ELTON JOHN CLAIMS AA ZOOM MEETINGS DURING PANDEMIC "A LIFESAVER"

Flash back to 2020, when Elton John wrote, "If I hadn't finally taken the big step of asking for help 30 years ago, I'd be dead." Superstar singer John admitted that his Alcoholics Anonymous (AA) meetings on Zoom were literally "a lifesaver" during the long dark days of the Covid pandemic.

"I'm a recovering alcoholic, so I have an AA meeting from this house every Sunday," the man who first crooned "Rocket Man" admitted on Prince Harry and Meghan Markle's new podcast called Archewell Audio. "I connect with my friends who I've known for about 30 years in the program, and that's great. If it hadn't been for Zoom, I don't know what we would've done. It's been a lifesaver."

Elton recalled that he was in the midst of a concert tour when the pandemic descended, and he was suddenly obligated to return home to Britain. "It was very strange because we were going full pelt," he remembered, "and then all of a sudden we ground to a halt."

It's a fact that John's in a higher-risk group for the virus since he's older, and also has an underlying condition. "I'm 73 years old, and I'm a semi-diabetic, so I'm in a risky area there," he explained. He added that even though he was able to see his husband and kids every day, he depended on trusty phone calls and Zoom to keep in touch with his extended family.

Elton commemorated 30 years of sobriety, writing on Instagram in July 2020: "Reflecting on the most magical day having celebrated my 30th Sobriety Birthday." He added, "If I hadn't finally taken the big step of asking for help 30 years ago, I'd be dead."

That's a sobering thought, Elton.

CHAPTER 69:

LOST DOGS RETURN HOME WHEN THE OWNER COOKS SPECIAL SAUSAGES

How could two adorable miniature schnauzers, Charlie and Theo, remain lost for four days in Cumbria, England? We may never know since their communication skills are somewhat limited. But we do know that the smell of their favorite sizzling sausages caused them to eventually return.

Liz and Graham Hampson were totally distressed when somehow their "fuzzy fur babies" disappeared on June 16, 2017. So, they did everything in their power to get their pups back. The couple's personal rescue campaign recruited friends, family, mountain rescue teams, and even a couple of drones.

All told, more than 120 people attempted to bring the darling pooches back. But more than 90 hours passed, and the dogs still didn't turn up. It was then that the family made their fateful choice and "decided to barbecue some sausages near the spot where they vanished, and shout the dogs' names."

The sausage campaign was a roaring success. Charlie and Theo came rushing through the trees soon after, and happily reunited with their human family. And let's not forget to thank the sausages, along with 120 others.

CHAPTER 70:

CANCER TRIAL'S UNEXPECTED RESULT: EVERY PATIENT IN REMISSION

They conducted a small trial, with only 18 rectal cancer patients, each one taking the same drug. However, the results were simply amazing. The previously detected cancer disappeared in every single patient - those bad cells were undetectable by physical exam, endoscopy, PET scans, and M.R.I.s.

Dr. Luis A. Diaz Jr., from the Memorial Sloan Kettering Cancer Center, authored a paper printed in the *New England Journal of Medicine* which described the results, sponsored by the drug giant GlaxoSmithKline. He did not know of any other study in which treatment had completely wiped-out cancer in every patient.

"I believe this is the first time this has happened in the history of cancer," Dr. Diaz exclaimed. In the meantime, Dr. Alan P.

Venook, a University of California colorectal cancer specialist in San Francisco, who wasn't involved in the study, stated that he thought it was a first also.

Total remission in every patient is "unheard of," he claimed. It's important to remember that these rectal cancer patients had faced grueling treatments as well - including chemotherapy, radiation, and probably, life-altering surgery that might result in bowel, urinary, and sexual dysfunction. In addition, some would need those cumbersome bags (called colostomy bags).

They all entered the study believing that, when it was all said and done, they'd have to submit to these hard procedures because nobody expected their tumors to vanish. But they got a nice surprise: No more treatment was necessary.

"There were a lot of happy tears," Dr. Andrea Cercek, a Memorial Sloan Kettering Cancer Center oncologist and co-author of the paper, recalled. The publication was presented at the annual meeting of the American Society of Clinical Oncology.

Another surprise, Dr. Venook noted, was that none of the patients had "clinically significant complications." On average, one in every five patients have some kind of adverse reaction to drugs similar to the one the patients received, Dostarlimab (also known as checkpoint inhibitors).

The medication was given every three weeks for six months, and cost about $11,000 per dose. It unmasks cancer cells, allowing the immune system to identify and destroy them.

One patient named Sascha Roth was expecting the worst. Yet after the trial, Dr. Cercek gave her the uplifting news. "We looked at your scans," she said. "There is absolutely no cancer." She didn't require any further treatment. "I told my family. They didn't believe me," recalled Ms. Roth. Yet a full two years later, she still doesn't have a trace of cancer.

CHAPTER 71:

STEPH AND AYESHA CURRY SERVE UP 15 MILLION PANDEMIC MEALS

You might guess that NBA superstar Steph Curry doesn't have a lot of time to spare. After all, he dribbles, flashes, sprints, and shoots his way through at least 100 pro basketball games a year. And wife Ayesha? She's plenty busy with her various professions: actress, author, blogger, model, TV personality, and YouTuber. Oh yes - she cooks a bit too.

Yet the celebrity couple still found the time to dish up some 15 million free meals to families in need since the Covid virus struck. A lot of folks are fans of the off-court and out-of-the-office charity of Steph and Ayesha Curry (though admittedly, many are even bigger fans of their cute kid, Riley).

The Chronicle reported to readers that the Currys' foundation 'Eat.Learn.Play.' was serving 300,000 meals a week to families in need in the East Bay area near San Francisco.

Soon after, the organization hit the million-meal milestone.

At last count, the foundation had served "well over 15 million meals" by their own admission. It's one of those programs that regularly pays struggling restaurants and food-adjacent businesses to fix free meals for families and the underemployed.

In their 2020 fourth quarter (no, not the latest Golden State Warriors basketball game) update, the program managed "to put back $20 million into the local economy," and was responsible for the rehiring of more than 900 Oakland restaurant workers.

Does this tale of Bay Area basketball nobility feeding millions of hungry people in a pandemic possibly get any more uplifting? In steps - chef José Andrés does. Chef Andrés' World Central Kitchen took advantage of a good-sized grant from the Curry Foundation to source meals from "more than 130 Oakland restaurants."

"It's like we're feeding the restaurants to make sure they can feed the community," explained Anna Shova, World Central Kitchen's restaurant operations head. "Restaurant culture has changed. Popular Michelin-star restaurants have now asked, 'What else can I do for the community?' Now, it's less about being rewarded, and more about being closer to the community. People are opening up their eyes."

The Curry's don't call the East Bay home anymore (they've moved to Atherton), but their involvement with the Oakland community was heart-warming. By the way, *Hoodline* reported that Ayesha Curry also decided to open a Sweet July retail store and café in Uptown Oakland. It carries the name of a lifestyle magazine she founded.

CHAPTER 72:

SAN ANTONIO PET STORE SELLS ONLY RESCUE CATS AND DOGS FROM 2020 ON

The San Antonio City Council voted 9-1 to stop the sale of dogs from breeders in the city's pet stores. Starting January 1, 2020, the city decided to only allow pet stores to offer dogs or cats they obtained from city or county animal shelters, animal control agencies, or animal rescue organizations.

What's at the heart of this issue: There's a current worry about so-called "puppy mills" - a phrase that animal rights activists use to refer to large, commercial breeding operations, in particular those that demonstrate poor conditions for animals and people alike.

"Most of the puppies being sold at pet stores are coming from out-of-state puppy mills or large breeders or brokers that pass the pets on from one state to another state," Heber

Lefgren, Director of Animal Care Services, informed council members.

A city of about 1.5 million folks, San Antonio has merely three pet stores within its city limits that sell dogs or cats: Petland, Puppyland, and Royal Pet Palace. The owners of the first couple spoke out in opposition to the ordinance at a meeting of the city council, defending their businesses and rights.

"You have it where you have good breeders and bad breeders. We understand that", Jaime Trueba, one of the Petland owners elaborated. "But obviously, we're working our best to get nothing but the good breeders. And what they're saying is that everything's bad across the board."

In the meantime, Lefgren admitted that none of the three pet stores has any reported violations with ACS, so there's no legitimate way to determine which of the suppliers from outside the city are truly good or bad as the market is "under-regulated."

"USDA standards do allow a breeder to confine a dog in a cage for its life that is six inches more than the size of the pet," Lefgren mentioned to the council. Imagine living in a house that stretches a bit further than your nose, and you get the idea.

ACS started to look at possible changes to pet sales in 2019. The city also put questions on the issue in two online surveys called SASpeakUp in July 2019 and February 2020. Lefgren admitted that the city didn't reach out directly to those stores, claiming "the voice of the pet stores is well-documented and well-known."

If there's any way that we can treat our pets better, before they even become our pets, we're all for it.

CHAPTER 73:

MISSING THREE-YEAR-OLD FOUND SAFE BESIDE A LOYAL DOG

An old (17 dog years, to be precise) blue heeler named Max stayed right by the side of a lost three-year-old girl, leading searchers to her after she survived more than 15 hours overnight in rugged bushland on Queensland's Southern Downs in Australia.

Aurora was reported missing at about 3:00 p.m. on a Friday after she wandered off on her own. But a search of woodlands and hills on the rural property in wet weather that same night found no trace of the girl.

The next morning, more than 100 State Emergency Service (SES) volunteers, police, and members of the public resumed the search and ultimately found the girl safe and well, together with Max the dog protector, at 8:00 a.m.

For his outstanding work keeping the little girl safe, Max was quickly declared an honorary police dog. Kelly Benston, the partner of Leisa Bennett, who is Aurora's grandmother, said Ms. Bennett and other searchers could faintly hear the tot from the top of a mountain on Saturday morning.

"She found the dog first. Max led her to Aurora," Mr. Benston said. SES area controller Ian Phipps confirmed that a family member spotted Aurora and Max about 1.2 miles from the house, still on the family property, at a place called Cherry Gulley, 18.6 miles south of Warwick.

"The area around the house is quite mountainous, and is very inhospitable terrain to go walking in, so she'd travelled quite a distance with her dog that was quite loyal to her," Ian said.

Ms. Bennett said she tracked her down after the three-year-old responded to her shouting. "When I heard her yell 'Grammy', I knew it was her," she exclaimed. "I shot up the mountain, and when I got to the top, the dog came to me and led me straight to her."

Ms. Bennett admitted that it was an emotional reunion with "a lot of tears." "I think [Aurora] was a bit overwhelmed by the tears and the howling, but I explained to her how happy those tears were," she enthused. "It could have gone any of 100 ways, but she's here, she's alive, she's well, and it's a great outcome for our family."

CHAPTER 74:

OZONE HOLE GETS SMALLER SINCE 1982, NASA CLAIMS

The ozone hole in our atmosphere was discovered back in 1982. In October 2019, our scientific friends at NASA said it was actually decreasing in size. Now, that doesn't necessarily mean we can run all over the place and celebrate with no clothes on. But it seems to be good news regardless.

That big offending hole in the ozone layer has diminished to its smallest size ever since scientists began checking it back in 1982. Part of this shrinkage is due to unusual weather patterns in the upper atmosphere over that fairly frigid place called Antarctica, said NASA. They'd like you to know that the cavity changes in size annually, and it's normally the largest during the colder months in the southern hemisphere, and from late September to early October.

The most recent glances at outer space show us that the hole spanned less than 3.9 million square miles at that point, constituting a record small size, almost half as large as it was during its peak at around 6.3 million on September 8, 2019. Specialists report that the hole is typically around 8 million square miles during this time of year.

Paul Newman (not the famous actor and salad dressing maker, mind you), the chief scientist for Earth Sciences at NASA's Goddard Space Flight Center, remarked that it's "great news for ozone in the Southern Hemisphere." At the same time, he advised: "It's important to recognize that what we're seeing this year is due to warmer stratospheric temperatures. It's not a sign that atmospheric ozone is suddenly on a fast track to recovery."

On the surface, the strengthening of the ozone layer seems to be a promising development - as it serves to protect the Earth more from harmful ultraviolet (UV) radiation that radiates from the sun. However, the news that the hole is shrinking isn't all good - the process that's closing the hole in the ozone is a clear product of an upsurge in global temperatures. But we'll take what we can get for now.

CHAPTER 75:

DOCTOR RUNS 22 MILES WITH A MASK TO PROVE OXYGEN'S THE SAME

We're happy to tell you that you really don't need to wear a mask to go out for a jog these days. But just for good measure, a U.K. doctor decided to run 22 miles to work and back, wearing a mask. He wanted to help stop the spread of misinformation and conspiracy theories around face coverings during the Covid pandemic while raising funds for charity.

The good guy and rapid runner is Tom Lawton. He works at the Bradford Royal Infirmary in Yorkshire (in the north of England) and said he ran with the mask on due to his overriding worries about people with respiratory illnesses. Those patients really wanted to wear masks but were afraid to because of false information.

After his run, he recorded that his levels of precious oxygen never fell below 98% of what they would usually be. As he informed *Newsweek*: "There are a lot of people out there who just don't want to wear a mask, and will find any excuse they can. But the people I'm more concerned about are people with respiratory illnesses, who would like to wear a mask, would like to do their bit, but are scared because there have been reports that it causes hypoxia [a condition where the body is deprived of oxygen]. I've seen some reports about people dropping dead while wearing masks.

"I'm someone who understands the science. I've got access to a pulse-oximeter [a device used to monitor the amount of oxygen carried around the body], so I can actually go out and show that it definitely doesn't. To make up for the fact that I'm fit and healthy, I thought if I'm running, then I'm using 10 times the amount of oxygen as I would if I'm just sitting here," Tom reasoned.

"If I can show that I can get 10 peoples' worth of oxygen through the mask, then hopefully someone who has a respiratory disease and wants to wear a mask, they can be reassured that it's a safe thing to do," the good doctor advised.

Tom also raised more than £2,400 for the Trussell Trust, a charity working to end "food poverty," and supporting food banks throughout the U.K. What exactly are some of the challenges of families who can't afford food? Lawton said, "It's something that has been a big problem for some time, and Covid-19 has unfortunately made it worse."

"I live in Bradford, one of the hardest-hit areas from Covid-19. It's an area where there's a significant ethnic minority population, there's a lot of deprivation, and it's really hard hit by Covid-19, and I hear reports from the food banks that the requirement has at least doubled for food banks in the area. So, I thought it'd be good to raise money," the running doc remarked.

As a result of the constant comparisons between the battle against Covid-19 and the Blitz Spirit that the British exemplified during World War II, he thought it important that just as people turned off their lights during the Blitz, and everyone tried to do their part to save the country, the same should happen in the fight against the virus.

"There are obviously people who can't wear masks for one reason or another, mostly for psychological reasons, or PTSD, but everyone who can do so really should. My mask protects you, your mask protects me," concluded Dr. Lawton.

Now that's the collaborative spirit, Tom.

CHAPTER 76:

JIMMY CARTER'S SOLAR PANELS POWER HALF HIS HOMETOWN

Once upon a time, when Jimmy Carter lived in a place called the White House in the U.S., he was the champion of new energy. He became the first president to use solar panels to provide power to parts of the famous building. That legacy continues decades later and now exists in a place much closer to Carter's home - literally speaking.

Since 2017, the country's 39th president has designated 10 acres of his farm to provide power to most of his hometown in Plains, Georgia. Where the famed farming president used to raise crops like nuts and soybeans, there currently stand 3,852 solar panels to capture the abundant Georgia sunshine. In turn, they take care of over 50% of the small town's energy.

The ex-president pointed out to the Sierra Club in 2017, just after the panels were set up, that "on a good day" they provided 1.3 megawatts, or 1.3 million watts. According to the U.S. government, one megawatt provides sufficient energy to power 400 to 900 homes (even though watts that come from solar panels provide a bit less).

In the words of SolAmerica, the firm that first contacted Carter about the idea, and then worked with him to install the panels on his farm, these nearly 4,000 solar panels are capable of providing more than 50% of the power needed by the 727 residents in this modest Georgia town.

SolAmerica Energy President George Mori told *PEOPLE* that the solar-panel farm continues to be operational "in its original size and still generates more than half the power in the town. SolAmerica has a partnership agreement with Georgia Power, the biggest electricity company in "The Peach State," which extends to 2042. It's expected that the panels will provide more than 55 million kilowatt hours of clean energy (we tend to like clean energy more than the dirty kind, don't we?) for the town of Plains.

"Distributed, clean energy generation is critical to meeting growing energy needs around the world, while fighting the effects of climate change," Carter stated. "I'm encouraged by the tremendous progress that solar and other clean energy solutions have made in recent years, and expect those trends to continue."

But wouldn't you know it: the Trump administration headed in the opposite direction, relaxing Obama-era restrictions on coal, and publicly decrying environmentally-friendly energy projects. Yet Carter isn't really new to butting heads with future presidents over green energy.

Soon after leaving the Oval Office in 1981, President Reagan came riding in and took down the solar panels Jimmy had installed at the White House. In the words of *Scientific American*, those very same solar panels are now spread around the world in museums as displays of the world's move toward more efficient energy.

One of them resides in the Smithsonian National Museum of American History in Washington, D.C., while another has a home in the Carter Presidential Library in Atlanta. You'll find more in China at the Solar Science and Technology Museum in Dezhou.

When he initially showed off the White House solar panels in June of 1979, Carter dedicated the future of energy to the public and challenged their willingness to embrace it. "A generation from now, this solar heater can either be a curiosity, a museum piece, an example of a road not taken, or it can be just a small part of one of the greatest and most exciting adventures ever undertaken by the American people," the peanut farmer proclaimed.

"When I told people we were getting solar panels, they said, 'In Plains?'" quipped Jan Williams, who used to manage the Plains Historic Inn Carter's hometown, in a 2017 *N.Y. Times* piece after the panels were first put up on his land. "They say, 'Well, that's because of Jimmy Carter.' It is because of Jimmy Carter. Plains is all because of Jimmy Carter."

It sounds like Jimmy was quite an important guy for the town of Plains and vice versa.

CHAPTER 77:

MAN GRADUATES FROM THE SAME UNIVERSITY WHERE HE STARTED AS A JANITOR

Frank Baez was a mere teen when he began to work as a janitor at the Langone Tisch Hospital at New York University. He kept bathrooms, hallways, and patient rooms sparkling clean. In May 2019, Baez (29) came full circle and graduated with a nursing degree given by the same institution where he started as a cleaner.

"I could barely speak English at the time when I started working at NYU," remembered Baez. That's because he moved to N.Y. from the Dominican Republic along with his mom at the tender age of 15. "Now I reflect on it, and I feel very proud of how much I accomplished."

Baez landed his first gig in hospital housekeeping because he was keen on getting a job that could help support his family. After he started working, he became increasingly interested in the medical field, and then applied for and was granted a job as a patient transporter, moving patients back and forth from their rooms to undergo surgeries and tests.

Baez ultimately left that job to wrap up his bachelor's degree at Hunter College nearby, thus becoming the first individual in his family to ever graduate from college. Yet the young man claimed he was always sure he wanted to get back to where he started: NYU.

"While working [at NYU] with the nurses, I realized I wanted to be one of them," said Baez. "I learned how much they advocate for their patients, and the passion they have for their job."

The janitor-turned-nurse was exhorted by the other nurses who worked with him to take a shot at NYU Rory Meyers College of Nursing. He was able to participate in an accelerated program that allowed him to graduate with a nursing degree in just 15 months.

"Our program is extremely rigorous," stressed Natalya Pasklinsky, the director of simulation learning at the college of nursing. "Frank didn't just kind of make the program, barely getting through. He flew through it with flying colors." We fully expect Mr. Baez to keep flying high for many years to come.

CHAPTER 78:

SMALL-SCALE TANZANIAN MINER GETS RICH OVERNIGHT, THEN BUILDS SCHOOL AND HEALTH CLINIC

A small-scale miner from Tanzania became a millionaire in a flash in June 2020, after he managed to sell two rough Tanzanite stones valued at $3.4 million. After that, he offloaded another gem for $2 million. The third discovery by the miner named Saniniu Laizer weighed 14 pounds. Now those are some whopping precious rocks.

Northern Tanzania happens to be the only place in this wide world where tanzanite is found, and it's mostly used to make ornaments. It also turns out to be one of the rarest gemstones on this planet. Furthermore, a local geologist estimated that the supply could be entirely wiped out in the next two decades.

What is this precious stone's appeal? Well, it has a rich variety of hues, including green, red, purple, and blue. And its value is determined by something referred to as "rarity" -the finer the color or clarity, the higher the price it fetches.

Laizer recommended that his fellow small-scale miners work with the government, saying that his experience was an example of a cooperative arrangement between an independent worker and the country's authorities. "Selling to the government means there are no shortcuts. They are transparent," he remarked at a ceremony near the northern mine of Mirerani.

Independent miners often gripe about the delayed royalty payments by mine owners, according to the BBC's Aboubakar Famau, speaking from the capital, Dodoma. (We're willing to bet that before reading this, nobody in your neighborhood knew the capital of Tanzania!)

After the June sale of his two rather large gems (weighing 20.28 pounds and 12.78 pounds), Mr. Laizer - who also happens to be the father of more than 30 children - told the BBC that he decided to host a "small party."

But he also promised that sufficient money would be donated to build a school and a health facility in his community in the Simanjiro district in northern Manyara.

The eminent miner told BBC that the windfall wouldn't change his lifestyle. He planned to continue caring for his 2,000 cows. He added that he didn't believe he needed to take any extra precautions because of his newfound funds.

There are other small-scale miners similar to Laizer who've acquired government licenses to seek out Tanzanite, but wildcat mining is widespread, especially close to mines that belong to big companies.

In 2017, Tanzanian president Magufuli made the military construct a 14-mile perimeter wall to seal off the Merelani mining site in Manyara, said to be the world's single source of Tanzanite. One year later, the government was glad to report a revenue increase in the mining sector and credited the rise to the wall's construction.

CHAPTER 79:

MICHAEL J. FOX RAISES $1 BILLION TO BEAT PARKINSON'S

Michael J. Fox decided to make a move to the U.S. from his native Canada around four decades ago. At the time, he was only thinking about one thing: being an actor. He hoped at least to land some commercial work.

Sure enough, he got into a McDonald's commercial in 1980, and eventually rocketed to fame as Alex P. Keaton on the TV Hit, *Family Ties*. Soon after, Michael became a huge box office draw with blockbuster films like *Back to the Future*. In his four decades in show biz, Fox has earned no fewer than five Emmys, two Golden Globes, and two SAG Awards.

But in 1991, at the tender age of 29, Fox was diagnosed with Parkinson's disease. Two years after making his diagnosis public, he created the Michael J. Fox Foundation for Parkinson's Research that helped pay for studies on therapies and cures. Since then, the organization has drummed up more than $1 billion in donations.

In October 2021, Fox celebrated the 20th anniversary of the foundation featuring his annual fundraising gala, "A Funny Thing Happened on the Way to Cure Parkinson's." Hosted by Denis Leary, the event took place at Jazz at Lincoln Center in N.Y. City, boasting a lineup that included Mike Birbiglia, Michelle Buteau, Lisa Fischer, Brad Paisley, and Sting.

"All I wanted to do was to book that McDonald's commercial," the 60-year-old Fox recalled about his early Hollywood days. "I didn't know I'd be trying to find a cure for Parkinson's." Though a cure for the condition might not be just around the corner, Fox affirmed that the foundation has had a direct impact on the progress of several vital therapies.

"They're therapies that have made life a lot better for a lot of people," Fox remarked. "I enjoy life more. I'm more comfortable in my skin than I was 20 years ago. I can sit down and be calm. I couldn't do that 25 years ago. That's the medications, the drug cocktails, and therapies that we've been a part of."

What's more: the organization's also boosted communication between patients and the medical and academic communities. Fox credits much of the success to the CEO and co-founder of the foundation, Deborah W. Brooks. "She's just magic," Fox enthused.

CHAPTER 80:

FLORIDA BEER-MAKER CREATES SIX-PACK HOLDER TO FEED TURTLES INSTEAD OF KILLING THEM

Have you ever seen those heart-breaking pictures of the damage that plastic six-pack rings can do to marine life? They mess with the wings of sea birds, choke seals, and damage the shells of growing sea turtles.

However, in 2019, a Florida brewery announced it had come up with a nice solution: six-pack rings that can either biodegrade or serve as a kind of snack for marine wildlife. After years of research and development, the rings - made simply of wheat and barley (some of the good stuff that goes in beer) - have popped up in stores in the southern part of the state.

Saltwater Brewery, a craft microbrewery located in Delray Beach, developed the rings together with EGPR, a local startup. But troubleshooting and manufacturing the rings turned out to be pretty expensive. Thus, E6PR hoped that other breweries, both big and small, would buy into the new rings and help lower the costs.

Plastic pollution is a large challenge for the Gulf of Mexico. According to recent research by Louisiana State University, the Gulf possesses one of the world's highest concentrations of marine plastic. Every net or bottle that was dunked into the Gulf by LSU researchers came up loaded down with plastic.

"We found it every time," LSU's Mark Benfield reported to *NOLA.com/The Times-Picayune*. In 2018, a volunteer beach cleanup effort along three miles of Elmer Island coastline turned up more than 170 six-pack rings made of nasty plastic, along with some 4,000 pounds of other garbage.

The amount of plastic currently in our oceans is not the uplifting part of the story. The fact that turtles and other marine creatures can now enjoy a biodegradable snack without harm is the real deal.

CHAPTER 81:

STUDENT WALKS 20 MILES FOR THE FIRST DAY OF WORK, SO BOSS GIVES HIM HIS CAR

When a youthful Birmingham college student's car quit working the night before he was supposed to start a new job, he didn't give up. Instead, Walter Carr decided to walk to work. He walked from Homewood to Pelham, Alabama. All night. In the dark. That's about 20 miles or more.

He's a Carver High School grad, and U.S. Marine hopeful. Carr kept walking throughout the early morning hours on Friday because he needed and really wanted, that specific job with Bellhop Moving. He made it to Hoover by 2 a.m. and then arrived in a place called Pelham at 4 a.m. (We imagine that you were still sleeping at that time.)

In Pelham, the young man's odyssey took a surprising turn. Four Pelham police officers showed their concern and kindness, which later was combined with publicly-posted words revealing the admiration and amazement of the moving company's clients. Carr's work ethic and clear dedication finally resulted in a very big pat on the back from Bellhop CEO Luke Marklin.

Marklin drove from Tennessee claiming he wanted to meet Carr for coffee to express his appreciation in person. That meeting ended with Marklin giving Carr a bit of a surprise when the boss handed the student the keys to his own practically new 2014 Ford Escape.

"I am honestly blown away by him,'' Marklin gushed about Carr. "Everything he did that day is exactly who we are - heart and grit. So far, he's batting 1,000." (Well, if you know anything about baseball, you know that's almost impossible.) Anyway, an emotional Carr had just one word when Marklin flipped him the keys: "Seriously?"

The compliments for Carr began on the weekend with a Facebook post from Jenny Lamey. She and her husband, Chris, got up at about 5:45 a.m. on Friday to get everything ready for the movers. At about 6:30 a.m., the doorbell rang, and the Lameys found a few Pelham police officers that had dropped by.

"He proceeded to tell us that he had picked up 'this nice kid' in Pelham early this morning. The nice kid, Walter, said that he was supposed to help us with our move today. It was his first day on the job with this moving company (Bellhop) and he was 'training' today," related Jenny Lamey.

The officers then informed the Lameys of Carr's persistence in arriving at work on time. This seems like the kind of person the U.S. Marines would welcome.

CHAPTER 82:

BETTY WHITE TURNS 99, AND CAN STAY UP AS LATE AS SHE WANTS!

Betty White turned 99 years old on January 17, 2021, and she seemed a bit philosophical: "I can stay up as late as I want, without asking permission." Her plans for the day? Feeding a couple of ducks that live at her L.A. home. What was on the menu? No ducks - just a hot dog and a few French fries, provided by her agent, Jeff Witjas.

Betty's show biz career began back in 1939. Most actors and actresses feel lucky if they have one gigantic hit during their careers. But after Betty scored her first, she didn't slow down. Her role playing Sue Ann Nivens on *The Mary Tyler Moore Show* was monumental. The show became one of the biggest hits in TV history.

She followed that with *The Golden Girls*, playing the character called Rose for eight years, and exactly 204 episodes. Another great show biz story involved the mobilization of admirers and fans that led to her hosting *Saturday Night Live* back in 2010.

Where did it all begin? Oak Park, Illinois, in 1922. She really wanted to be a forest ranger, but sadly women weren't allowed to get into that type of thing at the time. Betty married Allen Ludden, who was the daytime and prime-time *Password* host from 1963 to 1981.

Allen's opening catchphrase on the TV show - "Hi doll!" - was reportedly directed at Tess White, the mother of his wife, that classic actress and TV personality, Betty White.

CHAPTER 83:

955 GOLD MINERS ALL SAFE AFTER A 30-HOUR ORDEAL

Imagine you were planning to work your regular eight-hour shift, but you got stuck at your desk, for 30 hours instead! Now you have a better idea of what confronted a brave group of South African miners.

Every single one of the 955 gold miners who were trapped underground for more than a day in South Africa after a dramatic power cut came to the surface again, unharmed, on February 2, 2018, according to the mine's owner, Sibanye Gold.

"Everybody's out," announced spokesperson James Wellsted, who clarified that there were "cases of dehydration and high blood pressure, but nothing more serious."

The miners got trapped for almost 30 hours in the Beatrix gold mine, located in the small town of Theunissen close to the city of

Welkom, following a massive power outage caused by a storm. The disabled lifts were then unable to bring night-shift workers up to the surface.

After several hours, engineers managed to restore power, allowing the hoist to bring up the miners who'd been trapped since Wednesday evening in bunches. When asked if there'd been any casualties, Wellsted reported there was "no indication so far that anyone has been in distress," although it definitely had been a "traumatic experience."

Various ambulances arrived overnight at the site, an AFP reporter added. Nervous family members remained "patiently" together along the road to the mineshaft but were kept at a distance by security guards. The eventual reunions were no doubt glorious.

CHAPTER 84:

STOLEN CHARLES DARWIN NOTEBOOKS RETURNED 22 YEARS AFTER LAST SEEN

Two "stolen" or "borrowed" notebooks written by none other than Charles Darwin were mysteriously brought back to Cambridge University, 22 years after they'd last been seen. The smallish leather-bound books are valued at millions of British pounds and include the scientist's invaluable "tree of life" sketch.

Fifteen months after the BBC first highlighted that they'd gone missing, and the library launched a worldwide appeal to find them, they were magically returned in good shape. "I feel joyous," Dr. Jessica Gardner, the university librarian, said in celebration.

She grinned from ear to ear as she delivered the news. In fact, she couldn't stop smiling. "They're safe, they're in good condition, they're home." But who was the individual that returned the two postcard-sized notepads? It remains a real whodunit.

The notebooks were left, anonymously, in a bright pink gift bag, which contained the original blue box the notebooks were stored in, as well as a simple brown envelope. On it was found a short message: "Librarian, Happy Easter X." There inside were the two treasured notebooks, bundled tightly in cling film. The package was left on the floor, in a public section of the library that had no CCTV, just outside Dr. Gardner's office.

"I was shaking," admitted Dr. Gardner about her reaction to witnessing the bag and its precious contents for the first time on March 9. "But I was also cautious because until we could unwrap them, you can't be 100% sure."

A difficult delay of five days followed between the time the package was discovered and the police permitting them to open the cling film, check the notebooks carefully, and confirm they were authentic.

"There have been tears," Dr. Gardner sheepishly elaborated. "And I think there still will be because we're not over the emotional rollercoaster. It means so much to us to have these home."

She revealed her worst fear: that the notebooks might not be returned in her lifetime. "I thought it might take years. My sense of relief at the notebooks' safe return is profound and almost impossible to adequately express. I was heartbroken to learn of their loss, and my joy at their return is immense," Gardner expressed.

The notepads date back to the late 1830s after Darwin had just returned from the faraway Galapagos Islands, off the coast of Ecuador. On one of the pages, he drew a delicate sketch of a tree, which helped inspire his theory of evolution. More than two decades later, it would become a central theme in his revolutionary work, *On the Origin of Species*.

"The theory of natural selection and evolution is probably the single most important theory in the life and earth environmental sciences, and these are the notebooks in which that theory was put together," Jim Secord, emeritus professor of history and philosophy of science at Cambridge University, explained.

"They're some of the most remarkable documents in the whole history of science," the professor stated. Nice to have you back!

CHAPTER 85:

N.J. TEACHER LEAVES $1 MILLION IN A WILL FOR SPECIAL-ED STUDENTS

Some 10 years ago, Superintendent Emanuele Triggiano remembered having a laugh when a retired teacher informed him that she was going to donate a million dollars. "I thought it was a joke," Triggiano clarified. "But then we got the paperwork."

Genevieve Via Cava, a special education teacher in the Dumont (New Jersey, USA) school district, amassed a small fortune during her life. Upon her death in 2011, she donated her savings to help those people who truly meant the most to her: her special ed students.

"She was very kindhearted, sometimes with a rough exterior, but very compassionate deep down," remembered Richard Jablonski, a close friend and the executor of her will. "She was very loving, and won people over with her beautiful smile."

Beginning with the 2019-20 school year, a single special education student desiring post-high-school education, like college or a trade school, would be eligible for a $25,000 scholarship, courtesy of Via Cava's million-dollar gift.

The school district also intended to give a scholarship for the 2018-2019 school year, though it probably wouldn't be the full $25,000 amount, depending on the investment, according to Triggiano.

The money is destined to remain in a fund that generates interest, permitting the district to give out more scholarships for many years to come, Business Administrator Kevin Cartotto explained.

Via Cava had no kids and spent most of her career in the school district, involved in both regular and special ed. Her wish to pay it forward to help future generations came as no surprise at all to those who knew her well. Jablonski met Via Cava more than 35 years ago while operating an Annie Sez store in Closter.

Via Cava visited often with her husband and ultimately became a regular client. After her husband died in 1998, Via (who lived in

Oradell) continued to frequent the store, making friends with any and every person she ran into that day.

"She was an amazing woman who could light up a room just by walking in," Jablonski recalled. "She had an unbelievable smile. She could talk to anybody just to start a conversation with them, and by the time they walked away, they would be hugging."

CHAPTER 86:

IRANIAN CHAMP AUCTIONS OLYMPIC GOLD TO HELP EARTHQUAKE VICTIMS

An Iranian weightlifter won Olympic gold and then put his 2016 Rio medal up for auction to raise money for the victims of the horrific 7.3-magnitude earthquake that hit near the Iran-Iraq border in November 2017.

Kianoush Rostami, 26, spread the news on his Instagram account. More than 400 people perished in the quake, and almost 10,000 were injured. The western Iranian province of Kermanshah was the area most severely affected, with hundreds of homes destroyed, and many residents forced to suddenly sleep outside in the bitter cold.

Rostami, himself from Kermanshah, claimed he was "taking a step, however small" to aid those battered by the tremors. "I am returning my Rio 2016 Olympics gold medal -

which actually belongs to them - to my people," he stated in a widely-circulated Instagram post, adding that he'd been unable to sleep since the disaster.

"I will put my medal up for auction. All the proceedings will go to those hit by the earthquake." Rostami, of Kurdish ethnicity, also said he was teaming up with several other athletes to rally donations for the victims, posting a picture of himself in front of quilts, warm clothes, and water bottles.

Numerous Iranian Twitter users were quick to praise Rostami. "Amid all the bad news, Kianoush Rostami's announcement gave us hope," affirmed one tweeter. "He is gifting the public what he had earned to make them happy," tweeted yet another.

He wasn't the only prominent Iranian athlete who stepped up to help. Ali Daei, former captain of Iran's national football team who is also the globe's leading international scoring champion, jumped on social media to raise more funds for the worst affected.

In a video posted on Instagram, Daei assured followers he was setting up a bank account to collect donations, guaranteeing his myriad followers that the funds would directly go to the victims. "We can do so many great things if we stick together," he concluded.

CHAPTER 87:

WOMAN WHO CAN SMELL PARKINSON'S AIDS SCIENTISTS

Women are sometimes said to be more intuitive than men. And the fairer sex seems to be able to smell something when it's fishy as well. Here's an uplifting story about a wife who sniffed out her husband - not necessarily for bad behavior. Instead, she was able to give doctors a partial jump on her husband's treatment for Parkinson's disease.

A Scottish woman learned that she could detect Parkinson's through her sense of smell. She's since inspired scientists to create a swab test that can potentially be used to diagnose it. Manchester researchers have developed a new method that they claim can reveal the disease in only three minutes.

More studies are required to ascertain the findings before a diagnostic test that can be used in clinics or by General Practitioners (GPs) is delivered. Yet, all this work was inspired by Joy Milne, a retired nurse from Perth.

Joy, 72, realized that her husband Les had Parkinson's more than 12 years before he was officially diagnosed because she identified a change in the way he smelled. "He had this musty, rather unpleasant smell, especially round his shoulders and the back of his neck, and his skin had definitely changed," she recalled.

But she only connected the odor to the disease after Les was diagnosed, and they then met people at a Parkinson's UK support group who exhibited the same unique smell. Alas, Les died in June 2015. Later, a team at the University of Manchester, working with Joy, came up with a simple skin-swab test that they claim is 95% accurate under lab conditions in determining if people have Parkinson's.

The testers analyzed something called sebum - the oily substance on our skin - collected with a cotton swab used on patients' backs, an area where it's less often washed away (a little harder to reach when you take that long shower).

Through mass spectrometry, researchers compared 79 people with Parkinson's to a healthy control group of 71 folks. The research identified more than 4,000 distinct compounds in the samples, 500 of which were different contrasting people with Parkinson's and the control group.

Professor Perdita Barran, the research lead, admitted that there wasn't a chemical test currently for Parkinson's. Many thousands of people languished on waiting lists, hoping for a neurological consultation. She stressed that creating a confirmatory test that could be used by a GP would be "transformative."

"At the moment, we've developed it in a research lab, and we're now working with colleagues in hospital analytical labs to transfer our test results to them so that it can work within an NHS environment," she explained. "We're hoping within two years to be able to start to test people in the Manchester area."

Joy understands what an earlier diagnosis would've represented for her, and her family. "We would have spent more time with family," she remarked. "We would have travelled more. If we had known earlier, it might have explained the mood swings and depression."

One night before her husband died, he got her to promise to investigate her keen sense of smell. According to Joy, her husband said: "You must do this because it will make a difference." She really hopes her chance discovery will achieve exactly that.

CHAPTER 88:

FLORIDA MAN PAYS PAST UTILITY BILLS FOR 114 FAMILIES

A Florida business owner, who once rued his own lack of luck, decided to give back by shelling out for the utility bills of 114 families, all of whom were confronting disconnection.

Michael Esmond's generous streak started last year: he agreed to pay the utility bills of 36 households in his Gulf Breeze community. In 2020, both Hurricane Sally and Covid-caused economic turmoil crashed into the city. Esmond thought he needed to turn it up a notch.

"This year to me probably is more meaningful than last year, with the pandemic and all the people out of work having to stay home," Esmond informed CNN. "Hurricane Sally slammed us pretty good and hurt a lot of people. We still have a lot of the blue roofs here, where they're just covered with tarps."

In the end, Esmond donated $7,615.40 to cover the past-due bills of the 114 households, according to Joanne Oliver, the utility billing supervisor for the city. Holiday cards alerting the residents would be mailed that very week, she reported.

Michael's donation jumped up from the $4,600 he paid the previous year, and he said he could help about three times as many households. That's because many residents had bills to take care of valued at $100 or less, so he was able to help a greater number of people.

"That really impacted me - that people can't even afford to pay a $100 bill on their utilities, and things are so bad," Esmond exclaimed. "That's why I was able to pay for 114 families." The business turned out well in 2020 for 74-year-old Esmond, owner of Gulf Breeze Pools and Spas.

That's something he admits he's "almost ashamed" to tell people because he realizes how hard it's been for so many. "We've had a good year, and that's why I want to share what I have with the people who need it," Esmond declared.

CHAPTER 89:

FOUNDED BY UKRAINIANS, GRAMMARLY STILL PAYS STAFF WHO JOINED UKRAINE'S ARMY

With Russia's continued attacks on Ukraine, we've been trying to think of any and all ways we can help the Ukrainians. Now we know that one of the most successful tech startups in the USA is doing the same.

Grammarly Inc. decided to continue to foot the full salaries and benefits for its employees located in Ukraine who joined the country's army to battle against the Russian invasion, the company's CEO announced on March 21, 2022.

"The team is, first and foremost, focused on their safety," CEO Brad Hoover declared, refusing to specify just how many of his employees had joined Ukraine's defensive efforts. Before the war, almost half of

Grammarly's more than 600 staffers were based in Ukraine.

Hoover said many of those people had since left the embattled country or moved to areas inside Ukraine that were safer from conflict. Grammarly provides "a typing assistant" and was valued by investors at a cool US$13 billion in November of that year.

When the fighting started, its departments that had operations in Ukraine shifted the responsibility elsewhere within the company. Hoover initially spent a considerable amount of time on relocation and relief efforts. A majority of the company's Ukrainian workforce incredibly was back online despite the conflict.

Grammarly offered paid leaves of absence to workers who had no choice but to flee their homes, due to the fighting. "This is destroying people's lives," Hoover emphasized. "It's an incredible tragedy."

Rahul Roy-Chowdhury, Grammarly's global product head, stressed that the company hadn't changed its priorities as it formed second-quarter plans. Some progress on Grammarly's goals might be slower than previously expected, he admitted.

Grammarly's business has been profitable "pretty much since inception. We run ourselves like a public company," Hoover affirmed. "Because we don't need to IPO, we view that as something we can save for the future."

That profit helps the company give back to those in need - including those caught in the crossfire between Ukraine and Russia.

CHAPTER 90:

100K-STRONG KOREAN GROUP CHEERS FOR OTHER COUNTRIES

Could you put aside old grudges and cheer for your former foes? Most people might have a tough time with this task. But apparently not in Korea.

Not long after the Air Canada flight carrying Tessa Virtue and Scott Moir landed at South Korea's biggest airport, the Canadian figure skating pair found themselves greeted by a loud, happy throng.

Who on earth were those people showing off Canadian flags, and cheering with feverish energy suggesting they might even possess passports bearing the patriotic red maple leaf?

Most of them were by no means Canadians. Many were members of the Korean Supporters, a group of Korean volunteers who intended to dedicate their Olympic Games to a rather unusual mission: Cheering for countries that were not their own.

"Everyone else in Korea is going to support Korea. We're trying to focus on other countries," stated Ki Yang Cho, the head of communications for the Korean Supporters, speaking with the help of a translator.

Ki explained that the group, composed of about 100,000 registered members, was bringing 200 volunteers to Seoul's Incheon Airport most days of the week to gladly welcome Olympic athletes and tourists as they took their first baby steps on Korean soil.

They formed an assembly line of global goodwill. Soon after Virtue and Moir enjoyed their special moment earlier in the week, players on the men's hockey team from Russia experienced a similarly rambunctious welcome.

Once the Games kicked off, there were plans to designate squads of about 100 to 120 Korean Supporters to each event. The Supporters bought their own tickets and were encouraged to cheer in the language used by the athletes they were assigned to support.

"We're cheering in Russian, English, Chinese, and Japanese," enthused Ki. "We're going to have chants. We're going to call out phrases. We're going to wave flags."

Maybe even the flag of North Korea - normally illegal to display in South Korea due to the nuclear-standoff-induced discord between the neighbors. North Korea arrived at the Games with a small group of athletes - not to mention a 229-strong cheering squad chosen to pull for athletes from both Koreas.

The Korean Supporters simply wouldn't let old grudges spoil the spirit of their cause.

CHAPTER 91:

NURSE LEARNS BABY SHE TREATED 28 YEARS AGO IS A NEW COLLEAGUE

What comes around goes around: You never really know how small the world is until you find out that your new colleague is in fact that special baby you treated some 28 years ago.

While most of us haven't experienced anything similar, that's exactly what happened to intensive care nurse Vilma Wong. The 54-year-old was shocked to learn that the new doctor in the ward, Brandon Seminatore, was indeed a baby she'd nursed when he was born.

Vilma took care of Brandon when he was prematurely delivered at a mere 26 weeks. Vilma has worked in the neonatal intensive care unit (NICU) at Lucile Packard Children's Hospital in Palo Alto, California, for 32 years. When she spotted the young doctor's name, she instantly recognized it, but couldn't quite place where she'd seen it before.

When Brandon revealed to her that they both worked at the hospital in which he was born, she suddenly knew who he was. Brandon, specializing in child neurology, even had a picture of the two snapped in his early days.

"I got very suspicious because I remember being the primary nurse to a baby with the same last name," Vilma recalled upon seeing the doc's name for the first time. "I asked him if his dad was a police officer, and there was a big silence, and then he asked me if I was Vilma. I said yes.

"Apparently, his mother asked him to look for nurse Vilma in the NICU, but he told his mom that I'd probably retired by now. I was in shock initially, but overjoyed to know that I took care of him almost 30 years ago, and now he's a pediatric resident to the same population he was part of when he was born."

CHAPTER 92:

SHOPLIFTER STEALS CLOTHES FOR JOB INTERVIEW, BUT CANADIAN CONSTABLE BUYS OUTFIT, AND MAN GETS JOB

Have you been a positive role model in your community recently? All right - we'll forgive you if you're currently relaxing on the couch watching the game or the news.

But just so you know: In August 2017, a shoplifter in Toronto was nabbed stealing an outfit for a job interview. When Constable Niran Jeyanesan showed up to arrest him, he was moved by the 18-year-old's story and ended up buying him the clothes in question.

Later, the officer revealed that the young man actually got the job and would start working the following week. "He's starting Monday," Jeyanesan told Canada's *CP24* via email.

"He told me he actually wore the shirt and the tie - I'm just so happy!" Continued the officer, who then related how Walmart staff had busted the would-be thief for trying to steal a dress shirt, a spiffy necktie, and socks.

"This young person has been facing his own difficulties in life, and he was looking to straighten out all that by providing for his family and trying to get a job," Jeyanesan stated. "This individual didn't have any resources. He wanted to go get that job. That was in his mind. I think he truly made a mistake."

The teen told the officer that his father was ill and that the family had suffered some tough times as a result. Constable Jeyanesan also said that due to "some friends who were willing to help out," the father is now employed as well.

In an interview with the BBC, Jeyanesan's staff sergeant Paul Bois spoke highly of his actions. "Arresting him [the 18-year-old] wouldn't have been in the best interests of anyone," he declared. "I reacted very positively to the news; all issues were resolved by the action the officer took. It reiterates our goal of being positive role models in the community."

CHAPTER 93:

DYING PATIENT ASKS TO SEE THE OCEAN ONE LAST TIME, SO AMBULANCE MAKES A DETOUR

A pair of Queensland (Australia) paramedics arranged a detour to the beach for a palliative care patient who wanted to see the ocean once again. In November 2017, the unidentified patient was being transported to the palliative care unit of a local hospital when she mentioned her strong desire to see the beach.

The paramedics decided to take a slightly different route to the hospital, propping the patient up in the stretcher so she was able to see the ocean stretching out beyond beautiful Hervey Bay.

A Facebook post at the time nicely summed up the situation: "Tears were shed and the patient felt very happy.

Sometimes it is not the drugs/training/skills - sometimes all you need is empathy to make a difference! Great work, Hervey Bay team - Danielle & Graeme - the Service is very proud of you."

CHAPTER 94:

ARIZONA MAN FINDS MEXICAN GIRL'S WISH LIST ON BALLOON, THEN DELIVERS CROSS-BORDER GIFTS

We always wondered: what really happened to those carefully-crafted letters we wrote (and somebody possibly sent) to Santa Claus? Were you wondering the same?

This was a Christmas wish that crossed country borders. An Arizona man took care of the Christmas list of an eight-year-old girl in Mexico after her letter to Santa reached him by way of a balloon. (Her letter came up a bit short of Finland.)

Back in 2018, Randy Heiss was hiking in Patagonia, Arizona, when he spied the ragged remains of a balloon with a mysterious note attached. One side of the note read: "Dayami." The other showed a numbered list meticulously written in Spanish.

Heiss's wife was able to translate the list, and the couple identified its probable sender as a young girl named Dayami. The note was clearly intended for that jolly old fellow named Santa, and requested some art supplies, slime, a doll, and a dollhouse, among other things. No contact information was given on the note.

"It really touched my heart to find it, and I said, 'Well, how in the heck am I going to be able to figure out how to make contact with this little girl, and make her wishes come true?'" Heiss then informed the NBC affiliate KVOA in Tucson, thinking that the winds likely carried Dayami's Christmas wish list from Nogales, Mexico, about 20 miles away.

He shared the letter on Facebook, and after a few days with no leads, he enlisted the help of *Radio XENY*, a local station in Nogales. The station was kind enough to post Heiss's story on its Facebook page. Within an hour, they found Dayami living in Nogales.

The radio station told NBC News that it helped arrange for Heiss and his wife to meet Dayami and her family at its offices later that week. Heiss and his wife delivered the gifts to Dayami and her younger sister, Ximena, at the meeting. It brought him a dose of "healing joy" seeing the children's overjoyed faces, Heiss admitted on the *Today* show.

"Love has no borders," Heiss exclaimed. "That wall melted away for the day." As it turned out, the experience was a blessing for the pair too. "We lost our son nine years ago," Heiss told *KVOA*. "So, we don't have grandchildren in our future, and so really getting to share Christmas with kids was something that's been missing in our lives."

CHAPTER 95:

AFRICA DECLARED FREE OF POLIO

Did somebody once say that the best things in life are free? Now, the entire huge continent of Africa is finally free of that nasty condition called polio. In August 2020, Africa was declared free of wild polio by an independent body called the Africa Regional Certification Commission.

Polio usually affects children under the age of five, sometimes resulting in irreversible paralysis. Death can also occur when breathing muscles are impacted. Twenty-five years before, thousands of African children were paralyzed by the virus.

At this moment, the disease can still be found in Afghanistan and Pakistan. There's no cure, but the polio vaccine does protect children for life. Nigeria was the last African country declared free of wild polio, after having accounted for more than half of all global cases a short decade ago.

Nigeria's vaccination campaign entailed a huge effort to reach dangerous, remote places that were under constant threat from militant violence - some health workers were killed during the process.

Polio is a virus that moves from person to person, typically via contaminated water. It can lead to paralysis by assaulting the nervous system. Two out of three strains of wild poliovirus have been effectively wiped out worldwide. Now Africa has been declared free of the last remaining strain of wild poliovirus.

More than 95% of Africa's population has been immunized at this point. That was one of the conditions which the Africa Regional Certification Commission established before declaring the continent free of wild polio.

CHAPTER 96:

MAINE DOG MISSING FIVE DAYS FOUND ALIVE IN A SNOWBANK

Both people and dogs like to play in snowbanks, especially in Maine. One dog in "The Pine Tree State" played so much that she ended up lost for five full days. She was ultimately discovered - you guessed it - in a snowbank.

Sophie, a 13-year-old yellow Labrador retriever, was missing for five days. Albert Silver and his family, residents of Bryant Pond's Oxford County community, engaged the help of neighbors and the animal control officer in their frantic search for the dog, according to a *WCSH TV* report.

"We looked on foot and by snowmobile and by car," Silver related to the station. "We were pretty convinced that she had gone somewhere to die." At the time, the Silvers were participating in some of the other hobbies

Mainers like, such as plowing and shoveling snow when Sophie suddenly disappeared.

The Silvers' public post was shared more than 2,000 times. People the Silvers had never even met were looking high and low for Sophie. The search continued Friday, Saturday, Sunday, and then Monday. As the cold harsh nights marched on, Albert recalls they were quickly losing hope.

But then a sign, at 10 a.m. on Tuesday, right down the road from their house. Sophie's head miraculously appeared, poking out of the snow, showing the yellow lab completely buried and stuck in the yard of a camp the Silvers had previously checked.

It took a bit more plowing to reach her, but Sophie was not only alive, but she was also quite all right - after five full days in the cold, buried in snow. A preliminary check by the vet showed she'd lost five pounds but otherwise wasn't suffering frostbite or any serious injuries. (By the way, thanks Sophie for showing us all a new way to lose weight fast!)

Sophie could finally go home, where her family arranged a hero's welcome. Later online, "a thank you" note from Albert Silver appeared, addressed to the friends, family, as well as total strangers who searched valiantly for Sophie, and shared her photo. It all led to a most remarkable rescue.

CHAPTER 97:

FRUGAL IOWA CARPENTER HELPS 14 KIDS THROUGH COLLEGE

Don't you forget to pay it forward, like this modest Iowa carpenter who's been responsible for sending dozens of people to college? And these happen to be people he never had the chance to meet!

Dale Schroeder lived frugally his entire life. He grew up in poor conditions, never married or had kids, toiling as a carpenter at the same company for 67 years. He owned only two pairs of jeans and continued to drive an old, rusty Chevy truck.

Shortly before he died in 2005, Schroeder informed his attorney, Steve Nielsen, that he especially wanted to use his savings to help poor students in "The Hawkeye State" of Iowa make it to college. "I said, 'How much are we talking about, Dale?'" Nielsen told *KCCI*. "And he said, 'Oh, just shy of $3 million.' I nearly fell out of my chair."

Over the last 14 years, Schroeder's money has paid for 33 young Iowans to go to college. One weekend, they gathered around his old lunch box to speak of a man they'd never met, and how his generosity had truly changed their lives. "He wanted to help kids that were like him," Nielsen affirmed, "that probably wouldn't have an opportunity to go to college but for his gift."

One of those lucky kids was Kira Conrad. "I grew up in a single-parent household, and I had three older sisters, so paying for all four of us was never an option," said Conrad to *KCCI*. "[It] almost made me feel powerless, like, 'I want to do this, I have this goal, but I can't get there just because of the financial part.'"

Conrad remembers getting the call from Nielsen that her $80,000 tuition bill would be completely covered by a Schroeder scholarship. "I broke down into tears immediately," she recalled. "For a man that would never meet me, to give me basically a full ride to college, that's incredible. That doesn't happen."

Schroeder's account has recently run dry, but "Dale's Kids" - as the recipients call themselves - will always remember that quiet carpenter.

There was one small detail revealed as the students gathered. "All we ask is that you pay it forward," announced Nielsen. "You can't pay it back, because Dale's gone. But you can remember him, and you can emulate him."

The students have gone on to help others in a variety of fields: Conrad is a therapist while others became doctors and educators.

CHAPTER 98:

RWANDAN DRONE CUTS DELIVERY TIME FOR LIFE-SAVING MEDS

We've been looking forward to our next pizza delivery by drone. But check out this story: an innovative drone delivery service known as "Uber for Blood" has slashed the delivery time of life-saving medicines to remote regions of Rwanda. Deliveries that took four hours are now down to an average of 30 minutes. And the cargo is way more important than pizza!

A partnership between Zipline, a robotics company from Silicon Valley, along with the country's health ministry, has delivered more than 5,500 units of blood over the last year, frequently in life-threatening situations. The country's patients have never before received blood so quickly and efficiently.

While commercial drone delivery in wealthier countries is still in the testing phases, bogged down by busy skies and strict airspace regulations, Zipline delivers blood to 12 regional hospitals from an eastern Rwandan base. Each hospital serves up to half a million people.

The use of drones is also helping decrease maternal deaths - a quarter of which result from blood loss during childbirth - as well as high incidences of malaria-induced anemia, which is common in kids. In addition, drone delivery means hospitals need to store less blood, meaning less waste as blood spoils quickly.

Helping Tanzania is next on the list. "Some of the biggest, most powerful technology companies in the world are still trying to figure out how to do this. But East Africa is showing them all the way," said a Zipline spokesperson. "The work in Rwanda has shown the world what's possible when you make a national commitment to expand healthcare access with drones, and help save lives."

CHAPTER 99:

FRENCH NUN WHO SURVIVED WARS BEATS COVID BEFORE TURNING 117

If you should reach your 117th birthday, you too deserve a bite or two of baked Alaska for dessert.

A French nun who survived both world wars, and the 1918 flu pandemic, plus a coronavirus infection to boot, celebrated her 117th with red wine, a Mass in her honor, and then dinner, ending with her all-time favorite dessert: none other than Baked Alaska.

Sister André, believed to be the second-oldest person on the planet, was all set to spend her birthday commemorating her very long life at her care home in the French city of Toulon.

The facility spokesperson, David Tavella, told the Associated Press that the nun was "in great shape" and "really happy," with a busy schedule that featured a video call with her family, a service hosted by the Bishop of Toulon, and a champagne birthday feast.

"It's a big day," Tavella admitted, adding that there would be a cake for Sister André - although it clearly wouldn't be big enough to fit some 117 candles. "Even if we made big cakes, I'm not sure that she would have enough breath to blow them all out," he chuckled.

Tavella elaborated that the menu would include foie gras, capon with fragrant mushrooms, and a bit of alcohol to toast the occasion. "All of it washed down with red wine because she drinks red wine. It's one of her secrets of longevity. And a bit of Champagne with dessert, because 117 years have to be toasted," he insisted to the AP.

In the weeks prior to the big day, Sister André had to spend her days isolated in her room at the Sainte Catherine Labouré retirement home in the southern French city of Toulon. The nun was but one of dozens of the home's residents who tested positive for coronavirus.

But early in February 2021, Sister André was declared completely recovered from the virus, her retirement home informed Reuters, allowing her to maintain her title as "the oldest living European." This distinction came from the Gerontology Research Group's official "World Supercentenarian Rankings List." And so, the celebrations began!

CHAPTER 100:

REDUCED SHIPPING IN ALASKA LEADS TO HAPPIER WHALES

We couldn't resist ending our book of 100 uplifting stories by talking about a way to boost your happiness—and that of whales.

Covid caused Alaska's tourism to practically halt in 2020. Meanwhile, Christine Gabriele sat at her desk at the Glacier Bay National Park HQ in Gustavus, Alaska, and turned up the volume on her computer. The sweet sounds of gurgling and bubbling water filled the room. The calm was occasionally broken by the roar of a male harbor seal, looking to impress potential mates.

Gabriele's computer sat at the end of a five-mile underwater cable stretching into the bay's chilly waters, a national preserve swarming with fish, birds, sea otters, dolphins, unloved seals, and the area's star attractions - a few hundred humpback whales that migrate to

Alaska from the Hawaiian waters during the summer months.

For the past 18 months of the pandemic, there was something else she hadn't heard quite so much of - namely ships. During a normal summer, Glacier Bay and the surrounding area hums with traffic: every size of vessel, from the most massive, 150,000-ton cruise liners to smaller whale-watching boats, patrol the channels, all part of Southern Alaska's massive tourism industry.

The pandemic temporarily stopped all that. In 2019, more than 1.3 million people visited Alaska on ships. In 2020, there were just 48 - not even sufficient for an N.Y. City subway car! Overall, such marine traffic in Glacier Bay decreased by about 40%.

It took 12 minutes of listening to the soothing hydrophone audio in May to hear any trace of human activity - for example, the high-pitched whine of a boat propeller.

According to research by Gabriele, along with Cornell University researcher Michelle Fournet, the level of human-made sound in Glacier Bay the previous year dropped dramatically from 2018 levels, in particular at the lower frequencies generated by huge cruise ship engines. Peak sound levels were cut by almost half.

All of this allowed researchers to have an unfamiliar opportunity to study whale behavior in a quiet environment that hadn't existed in the area for at least a century. By analyzing the hydrophone data and using a small park service boat in Glacier Bay three times a week to identify and photograph whales, Gabriele already noted major changes.

She compared the whales' activity in pre-pandemic times to the human behavior seen in a crowded bar. They talked louder, they kept closer together, and they insisted on simple conversation.

At the time of the pandemic, humpbacks seemed to be spreading out across larger pieces of the bay. Whales were able to hear each other over a distance of 1.4 miles, compared with pre-pandemic distances closer to 650 feet.

All of a sudden, whale mothers were able to leave their calves to play while they swam out to feed. Some were observed taking naps. And whale songs - those weird whoops and pops by which the creatures communicate - became more and more diverse.

Gabriele acknowledged that the break in tourism caused by Covid was only temporary. And she hoped her research - and the long-standing efforts to control ship traffic in Glacier Bay - would allow a good balance to be found between the natural environment and the human desire to witness, and of course, to be inspired by, nature's incredible grandeur (and a bunch of happy whales).

CONCLUSION

That brings us to the end (for now) of our 100 uplifting stories, especially for those special seniors - our elders (and "wisers," if we may use the term) - among us. It's amazing to think how much experience and wisdom (and how many funny stories) our favorite elderly folks can share with us.

The stories herein that we've chosen are all meant to lift you and your families. They were specifically selected to encourage and inspire, and improve your lives, if only in some tiny way.

The uplifting tales here involve a great variety of feel-good subjects, like altruism and helping others, more heroism and justice in the world, as well as unbelievable longevity, fantastic philanthropic deeds, and a better work-life balance.

We hope that even the upbeat stories about more serious topics, like climate change action and environmental protection, will give you a little kick. Share the stories you like, and maybe somebody else will be lifted as well.